60 Muffins and Cupcakes Recipes for Home

By: Kelly Johnson

Table of Contents

Classic Muffins:

- Blueberry Muffins
- Banana Nut Muffins
- Chocolate Chip Muffins
- Lemon Poppy Seed Muffins
- Cranberry Orange Muffins
- Apple Cinnamon Muffins

Healthy and Wholesome Muffins:
- Whole Wheat Carrot Muffins
- Oatmeal Raisin Muffins
- Zucchini Muffins
- Spinach and Feta Muffins
- Pumpkin Spice Muffins
- Almond Flour Banana Muffins

Decadent Chocolate Cupcakes:
- Classic Chocolate Cupcakes
- Double Chocolate Chip Cupcakes
- Chocolate Peanut Butter Cupcakes
- Chocolate Mint Cupcakes
- Chocolate Espresso Cupcakes
- Dark Chocolate Raspberry Cupcakes

Fruity Cupcakes:
- Strawberry Cupcakes
- Raspberry Lemonade Cupcakes
- Mango Coconut Cupcakes
- Pineapple Upside-Down Cupcakes
- Peach Cobbler Cupcakes
- Blackberry Vanilla Cupcakes

Gourmet Flavors:
- Salted Caramel Cupcakes
- Red Velvet Cupcakes

- Pistachio Cupcakes
- Lavender Honey Cupcakes
- Matcha Green Tea Cupcakes
- Earl Grey Cupcakes with Lemon Frosting

Seasonal Specials:
- Spiced Apple Cider Cupcakes
- Pumpkin Cheesecake Cupcakes
- Gingerbread Cupcakes
- Cranberry White Chocolate Cupcakes
- Peppermint Mocha Cupcakes
- Eggnog Cupcakes

Nutty Goodness:
- Pecan Pie Cupcakes
- Almond Joy Cupcakes
- Hazelnut Chocolate Cupcakes
- Pistachio Rose Cupcakes
- Maple Walnut Cupcakes
- Peanut Butter Banana Cupcakes

Cupcake and Muffin Combinations:
- Blueberry Cheesecake Muffins
- Chocolate Chip Cookie Dough Cupcakes
- Lemon Blueberry Swirl Cupcakes
- Raspberry Almond Muffins
- Cinnamon Roll Cupcakes
- S'mores Muffins

Unique and Creative:
- Margarita Cupcakes
- Caramel Macchiato Cupcakes
- Chai Spiced Muffins
- Bacon Maple Pancake Cupcakes
- Sweet Potato Pecan Cupcakes
- Cucumber Mint Cupcakes with Gin Frosting

Gluten-Free and Vegan Options:
- Gluten-Free Blueberry Almond Muffins

- Vegan Chocolate Chip Banana Muffins
- Gluten-Free Lemon Coconut Cupcakes
- Vegan Pumpkin Spice Cupcakes
- Gluten-Free Zucchini Chocolate Muffins
- Vegan Vanilla Raspberry Cupcakes

Classic Muffins:

Blueberry Muffins

Ingredients:

- 2 cups all-purpose flour
- 1 cup granulated sugar
- 1 tablespoon baking powder
- 1/2 teaspoon salt
- 1/2 cup unsalted butter, melted
- 2 large eggs
- 1 cup milk
- 1 teaspoon vanilla extract
- 1 1/2 cups fresh or frozen blueberries (if using frozen, do not thaw)

Instructions:

Preheat Oven:
- Preheat your oven to 375°F (190°C). Line a muffin tin with paper liners or grease the cups.

Mix Dry Ingredients:
- In a large bowl, whisk together the flour, sugar, baking powder, and salt.

Combine Wet Ingredients:
- In a separate bowl, whisk together the melted butter, eggs, milk, and vanilla extract.

Combine Wet and Dry Ingredients:
- Pour the wet ingredients into the bowl of dry ingredients. Stir until just combined. Do not overmix; it's okay if there are a few lumps.

Add Blueberries:
- Gently fold in the blueberries until evenly distributed throughout the batter.

Fill Muffin Cups:
- Divide the batter evenly among the muffin cups, filling each about two-thirds full.

Bake:
- Bake in the preheated oven for 18-22 minutes or until the tops are golden and a toothpick inserted into the center comes out clean.

Cool:

- Allow the blueberry muffins to cool in the muffin tin for 5 minutes, then transfer them to a wire rack to cool completely.

Serve and Enjoy:

- Once cooled, serve and enjoy these classic blueberry muffins with your favorite beverage.

Tips:

- Tossing the blueberries in a little flour before folding them into the batter can help prevent them from sinking to the bottom during baking.
- If using frozen blueberries, be mindful that they may release more moisture into the batter. Adjust baking time as needed.

These blueberry muffins are a timeless favorite, perfect for breakfast or as a sweet treat any time of the day!

Banana Nut Muffins

Ingredients:

- 2 to 3 ripe bananas, mashed
- 1/2 cup unsalted butter, melted
- 1 teaspoon vanilla extract
- 1/2 cup granulated sugar
- 1/4 cup brown sugar, packed
- 1 large egg
- 1 1/2 cups all-purpose flour
- 1 teaspoon baking soda
- 1/2 teaspoon baking powder
- 1/4 teaspoon salt
- 1/2 teaspoon ground cinnamon
- 1/2 cup chopped nuts (walnuts or pecans), optional

Instructions:

Preheat Oven:
- Preheat your oven to 350°F (175°C). Line a muffin tin with paper liners or grease the cups.

Mix Wet Ingredients:
- In a large bowl, mash the ripe bananas with a fork. Add melted butter, vanilla extract, granulated sugar, brown sugar, and the egg. Mix well.

Combine Dry Ingredients:
- In a separate bowl, whisk together the flour, baking soda, baking powder, salt, and ground cinnamon.

Combine Wet and Dry Ingredients:
- Add the dry ingredients to the wet ingredients. Stir until just combined. Be careful not to overmix.

Add Nuts (Optional):
- If using nuts, fold in the chopped nuts into the batter.

Fill Muffin Cups:
- Divide the batter evenly among the muffin cups, filling each about two-thirds full.

Bake:
- Bake in the preheated oven for 20-25 minutes or until a toothpick inserted into the center comes out clean.

Cool:
- Allow the banana nut muffins to cool in the muffin tin for 5 minutes, then transfer them to a wire rack to cool completely.

Serve and Enjoy:
- Once cooled, serve and enjoy these delicious and moist banana nut muffins!

Tips:

- Overripe bananas with brown spots are perfect for extra sweetness and flavor in the muffins.
- If you prefer a nut-free version, feel free to omit the nuts or replace them with chocolate chips for a different twist.
- These muffins are great for breakfast or as a snack, and they freeze well for future enjoyment.

Enjoy these banana nut muffins with a cup of coffee or tea for a delightful and satisfying treat!

Chocolate Chip Muffins

Ingredients:

- 2 cups all-purpose flour
- 1/2 cup granulated sugar
- 1/4 cup brown sugar, packed
- 1 tablespoon baking powder
- 1/2 teaspoon salt
- 1 cup milk
- 1/2 cup unsalted butter, melted
- 2 large eggs
- 1 teaspoon vanilla extract
- 1 1/2 cups chocolate chips (semi-sweet or milk chocolate)

Instructions:

Preheat Oven:
- Preheat your oven to 375°F (190°C). Line a muffin tin with paper liners or grease the cups.

Mix Dry Ingredients:
- In a large bowl, whisk together the flour, granulated sugar, brown sugar, baking powder, and salt.

Combine Wet Ingredients:
- In another bowl, whisk together the melted butter, eggs, milk, and vanilla extract.

Combine Wet and Dry Ingredients:
- Pour the wet ingredients into the bowl of dry ingredients. Stir until just combined. Do not overmix.

Add Chocolate Chips:
- Gently fold in the chocolate chips until evenly distributed throughout the batter.

Fill Muffin Cups:
- Divide the batter evenly among the muffin cups, filling each about two-thirds full.

Bake:
- Bake in the preheated oven for 18-20 minutes or until a toothpick inserted into the center comes out with moist crumbs (not wet batter).

Cool:

- Allow the chocolate chip muffins to cool in the muffin tin for 5 minutes, then transfer them to a wire rack to cool completely.

Serve and Enjoy:
- Once cooled, serve and enjoy these classic chocolate chip muffins!

Tips:

- Feel free to use mini chocolate chips for a more evenly distributed chocolatey flavor.
- If you'd like a muffin top, slightly overfill the muffin cups.
- You can add a sprinkle of sugar on top of the muffins before baking for a sweet crunch.

These chocolate chip muffins are a delightful treat for breakfast or as a snack. Enjoy them warm with a glass of milk or your favorite hot beverage!

Lemon Poppy Seed Muffins

Ingredients:

- 2 cups all-purpose flour
- 3/4 cup granulated sugar
- 2 tablespoons poppy seeds
- 2 teaspoons baking powder
- 1/2 teaspoon baking soda
- 1/4 teaspoon salt
- 1 cup buttermilk
- 1/2 cup unsalted butter, melted
- 2 large eggs
- Zest of 2 lemons
- 3 tablespoons fresh lemon juice
- 1 teaspoon vanilla extract

Lemon Glaze:

- 1 cup powdered sugar
- 2-3 tablespoons fresh lemon juice

Instructions:

Preheat Oven:
- Preheat your oven to 375°F (190°C). Line a muffin tin with paper liners or grease the cups.

Mix Dry Ingredients:
- In a large bowl, whisk together the flour, sugar, poppy seeds, baking powder, baking soda, and salt.

Combine Wet Ingredients:
- In another bowl, whisk together the buttermilk, melted butter, eggs, lemon zest, lemon juice, and vanilla extract.

Combine Wet and Dry Ingredients:
- Pour the wet ingredients into the bowl of dry ingredients. Stir until just combined. Do not overmix.

Fill Muffin Cups:

- Divide the batter evenly among the muffin cups, filling each about two-thirds full.

Bake:
- Bake in the preheated oven for 18-20 minutes or until a toothpick inserted into the center comes out clean.

Cool:
- Allow the lemon poppy seed muffins to cool in the muffin tin for 5 minutes, then transfer them to a wire rack to cool completely.

Prepare Lemon Glaze:
- In a small bowl, whisk together the powdered sugar and fresh lemon juice until smooth.

Drizzle Glaze:
- Once the muffins are completely cooled, drizzle the lemon glaze over the top.

Serve and Enjoy:
- Serve and enjoy these moist and citrusy lemon poppy seed muffins!

Tips:

- Adjust the amount of lemon juice in the glaze to achieve your desired consistency.
- For an extra burst of flavor, you can add additional lemon zest to the glaze.
- Store the muffins in an airtight container at room temperature for freshness.

These lemon poppy seed muffins are perfect for a light and refreshing breakfast or snack. Enjoy the delightful combination of citrus and poppy seeds!

Cranberry Orange Muffins

Ingredients:

- 2 cups all-purpose flour
- 3/4 cup granulated sugar
- 1 tablespoon baking powder
- 1/2 teaspoon baking soda
- 1/4 teaspoon salt
- 1 cup fresh or frozen cranberries, coarsely chopped
- Zest of 1 orange
- 1/2 cup unsalted butter, melted
- 1 cup orange juice (freshly squeezed if possible)
- 2 large eggs
- 1 teaspoon vanilla extract

Orange Glaze:

- 1 cup powdered sugar
- 2-3 tablespoons fresh orange juice

Instructions:

Preheat Oven:
- Preheat your oven to 375°F (190°C). Line a muffin tin with paper liners or grease the cups.

Mix Dry Ingredients:
- In a large bowl, whisk together the flour, sugar, baking powder, baking soda, and salt.

Add Cranberries and Orange Zest:
- Stir in the chopped cranberries and orange zest into the dry ingredients until well combined.

Combine Wet Ingredients:
- In another bowl, whisk together the melted butter, orange juice, eggs, and vanilla extract.

Combine Wet and Dry Ingredients:
- Pour the wet ingredients into the bowl of dry ingredients. Stir until just combined. Do not overmix.

Fill Muffin Cups:
- Divide the batter evenly among the muffin cups, filling each about two-thirds full.

Bake:
- Bake in the preheated oven for 18-20 minutes or until a toothpick inserted into the center comes out clean.

Cool:
- Allow the cranberry orange muffins to cool in the muffin tin for 5 minutes, then transfer them to a wire rack to cool completely.

Prepare Orange Glaze:
- In a small bowl, whisk together the powdered sugar and fresh orange juice until smooth.

Drizzle Glaze:
- Once the muffins are completely cooled, drizzle the orange glaze over the top.

Serve and Enjoy:
- Serve and savor these delightful cranberry orange muffins!

Tips:

- If using frozen cranberries, you can fold them into the batter without thawing.
- Adjust the thickness of the glaze by adding more or less orange juice to achieve your desired consistency.
- Garnish the muffins with additional orange zest for a burst of citrus flavor.

These cranberry orange muffins are a perfect blend of tart cranberries and citrusy orange, making them a delightful treat for breakfast or snack time!

Apple Cinnamon Muffins

Ingredients:

- 2 cups all-purpose flour
- 1/2 cup granulated sugar
- 1/2 cup brown sugar, packed
- 2 teaspoons baking powder
- 1/2 teaspoon baking soda
- 1/2 teaspoon salt
- 1 teaspoon ground cinnamon
- 1/2 cup unsalted butter, melted
- 2 large eggs
- 1 cup unsweetened applesauce
- 1 teaspoon vanilla extract
- 1 1/2 cups diced apples (peeled and cored)

Cinnamon Sugar Topping:

- 2 tablespoons granulated sugar
- 1/2 teaspoon ground cinnamon

Instructions:

Preheat Oven:
- Preheat your oven to 375°F (190°C). Line a muffin tin with paper liners or grease the cups.

Mix Dry Ingredients:
- In a large bowl, whisk together the flour, granulated sugar, brown sugar, baking powder, baking soda, salt, and ground cinnamon.

Combine Wet Ingredients:
- In another bowl, whisk together the melted butter, eggs, applesauce, and vanilla extract.

Combine Wet and Dry Ingredients:
- Pour the wet ingredients into the bowl of dry ingredients. Stir until just combined. Do not overmix.

Fold in Diced Apples:
- Gently fold in the diced apples until evenly distributed throughout the batter.

Fill Muffin Cups:
- Divide the batter evenly among the muffin cups, filling each about two-thirds full.

Prepare Cinnamon Sugar Topping:
- In a small bowl, mix together the granulated sugar and ground cinnamon for the topping.

Sprinkle Topping:
- Sprinkle the cinnamon sugar topping over the batter in each muffin cup.

Bake:
- Bake in the preheated oven for 18-20 minutes or until a toothpick inserted into the center comes out clean.

Cool:
- Allow the apple cinnamon muffins to cool in the muffin tin for 5 minutes, then transfer them to a wire rack to cool completely.

Serve and Enjoy:
- Once cooled, serve and enjoy these deliciously spiced apple cinnamon muffins!

Tips:

- Use a mix of sweet and tart apples for a well-balanced flavor in the muffins.
- If desired, you can add a handful of chopped nuts (such as walnuts or pecans) to the batter for extra texture.
- These muffins are best enjoyed warm, but they can be stored in an airtight container for a few days.

These apple cinnamon muffins are a delightful fall treat, combining the warmth of cinnamon with the sweetness of apples for a perfect breakfast or snack!

Healthy and Wholesome Muffins:
Whole Wheat Carrot Muffins

Ingredients:

- 1 1/2 cups whole wheat flour
- 1/2 cup all-purpose flour
- 1 teaspoon baking powder
- 1/2 teaspoon baking soda
- 1/2 teaspoon salt
- 1 teaspoon ground cinnamon
- 1/2 teaspoon ground nutmeg
- 1/2 cup unsalted butter, melted
- 1/2 cup brown sugar, packed
- 1/4 cup honey
- 2 large eggs
- 1 teaspoon vanilla extract
- 1 1/2 cups grated carrots (about 3 medium carrots)
- 1/2 cup raisins or chopped nuts (optional)

Instructions:

Preheat Oven:
- Preheat your oven to 350°F (175°C). Line a muffin tin with paper liners or grease the cups.

Mix Dry Ingredients:
- In a large bowl, whisk together the whole wheat flour, all-purpose flour, baking powder, baking soda, salt, ground cinnamon, and ground nutmeg.

Combine Wet Ingredients:
- In another bowl, whisk together the melted butter, brown sugar, honey, eggs, and vanilla extract.

Combine Wet and Dry Ingredients:
- Pour the wet ingredients into the bowl of dry ingredients. Stir until just combined. Do not overmix.

Fold in Carrots and Optional Add-Ins:
- Gently fold in the grated carrots and raisins or chopped nuts (if using) until evenly distributed throughout the batter.

Fill Muffin Cups:

- Divide the batter evenly among the muffin cups, filling each about two-thirds full.

Bake:
- Bake in the preheated oven for 18-20 minutes or until a toothpick inserted into the center comes out clean.

Cool:
- Allow the whole wheat carrot muffins to cool in the muffin tin for 5 minutes, then transfer them to a wire rack to cool completely.

Serve and Enjoy:
- Once cooled, serve and enjoy these wholesome whole wheat carrot muffins!

Tips:

- Grate the carrots finely for a more even distribution throughout the muffins.
- If you're a fan of added texture, consider incorporating chopped nuts like walnuts or pecans.
- These muffins are versatile; you can customize them by adding ingredients like shredded coconut or dried fruits.

These whole wheat carrot muffins offer a nutritious and flavorful option for a snack or breakfast, perfect for those looking for a wholesome treat.

Oatmeal Raisin Muffins

Ingredients:

- 1 cup old-fashioned rolled oats
- 1 cup buttermilk
- 1 cup all-purpose flour
- 1 teaspoon baking powder
- 1/2 teaspoon baking soda
- 1/2 teaspoon salt
- 1 teaspoon ground cinnamon
- 1/2 cup unsalted butter, melted
- 1/2 cup brown sugar, packed
- 1/4 cup granulated sugar
- 2 large eggs
- 1 teaspoon vanilla extract
- 1 cup raisins

Instructions:

Preheat Oven:
- Preheat your oven to 375°F (190°C). Line a muffin tin with paper liners or grease the cups.

Soak Oats in Buttermilk:
- In a bowl, combine the rolled oats and buttermilk. Allow them to soak for about 15-20 minutes.

Mix Dry Ingredients:
- In a separate bowl, whisk together the flour, baking powder, baking soda, salt, and ground cinnamon.

Combine Wet Ingredients:
- In another bowl, mix together the melted butter, brown sugar, granulated sugar, eggs, and vanilla extract.

Combine Wet and Dry Ingredients:
- Add the wet ingredients to the dry ingredients, stirring until just combined.

Fold in Oat Mixture and Raisins:
- Gently fold in the soaked oat mixture and raisins until evenly distributed throughout the batter.

Fill Muffin Cups:

- Divide the batter evenly among the muffin cups, filling each about two-thirds full.

Bake:
- Bake in the preheated oven for 18-20 minutes or until a toothpick inserted into the center comes out clean.

Cool:
- Allow the oatmeal raisin muffins to cool in the muffin tin for 5 minutes, then transfer them to a wire rack to cool completely.

Serve and Enjoy:
- Once cooled, serve and enjoy these hearty and flavorful oatmeal raisin muffins!

Tips:

- You can add a handful of chopped nuts, such as walnuts or pecans, for added texture and flavor.
- For extra sweetness, consider drizzling a simple glaze made of powdered sugar and milk over the cooled muffins.

These oatmeal raisin muffins provide a wholesome and satisfying breakfast or snack option, combining the heartiness of oats with the sweetness of raisins.

Zucchini Muffins

Ingredients:

- 2 cups grated zucchini (about 2 medium-sized zucchinis)
- 2 cups all-purpose flour
- 1/2 cup granulated sugar
- 1/2 cup brown sugar, packed
- 1 teaspoon baking powder
- 1/2 teaspoon baking soda
- 1/2 teaspoon salt
- 1 teaspoon ground cinnamon
- 1/2 teaspoon ground nutmeg
- 1/2 cup unsalted butter, melted
- 2 large eggs
- 1 teaspoon vanilla extract
- 1/2 cup chopped nuts (walnuts or pecans), optional

Instructions:

Preheat Oven:
- Preheat your oven to 350°F (175°C). Line a muffin tin with paper liners or grease the cups.

Grate Zucchini:
- Grate the zucchini using a box grater and set aside. If the zucchini is very watery, you can place it in a clean kitchen towel and squeeze out some of the excess moisture.

Mix Dry Ingredients:
- In a large bowl, whisk together the flour, granulated sugar, brown sugar, baking powder, baking soda, salt, ground cinnamon, and ground nutmeg.

Combine Wet Ingredients:
- In another bowl, mix together the melted butter, eggs, and vanilla extract.

Combine Wet and Dry Ingredients:
- Add the wet ingredients to the dry ingredients, stirring until just combined.

Fold in Grated Zucchini and Nuts:
- Gently fold in the grated zucchini and chopped nuts (if using) until evenly distributed throughout the batter.

Fill Muffin Cups:

- Divide the batter evenly among the muffin cups, filling each about two-thirds full.

Bake:
- Bake in the preheated oven for 18-20 minutes or until a toothpick inserted into the center comes out clean.

Cool:
- Allow the zucchini muffins to cool in the muffin tin for 5 minutes, then transfer them to a wire rack to cool completely.

Serve and Enjoy:
- Once cooled, serve and enjoy these moist and flavorful zucchini muffins!

Tips:

- For a bit of added sweetness, you can include 1/2 cup of chocolate chips in the batter.
- Feel free to experiment with spices; a pinch of cloves or ginger can complement the cinnamon and nutmeg.
- These muffins can be frozen for longer storage. Ensure they are completely cooled before freezing.

These zucchini muffins are a great way to incorporate vegetables into a tasty treat, and they make for a wonderful breakfast or snack option!

Spinach and Feta Muffins

Ingredients:

- 2 cups fresh spinach, chopped
- 1 cup crumbled feta cheese
- 2 cups all-purpose flour
- 1 tablespoon baking powder
- 1/2 teaspoon baking soda
- 1/2 teaspoon salt
- 1/4 teaspoon black pepper
- 1/2 cup unsalted butter, melted
- 1 cup buttermilk
- 2 large eggs
- 1 teaspoon dried oregano or Italian seasoning
- 1/2 cup grated Parmesan cheese (optional, for topping)

Instructions:

Preheat Oven:
- Preheat your oven to 375°F (190°C). Line a muffin tin with paper liners or grease the cups.

Prepare Spinach and Feta:
- In a skillet, sauté the chopped spinach over medium heat until wilted. Allow it to cool, then combine it with crumbled feta in a bowl.

Mix Dry Ingredients:
- In a large bowl, whisk together the flour, baking powder, baking soda, salt, and black pepper.

Combine Wet Ingredients:
- In another bowl, mix together the melted butter, buttermilk, eggs, and dried oregano.

Combine Wet and Dry Ingredients:
- Add the wet ingredients to the dry ingredients, stirring until just combined.

Add Spinach and Feta:
- Gently fold in the sautéed spinach and feta mixture until evenly distributed throughout the batter.

Fill Muffin Cups:

- Divide the batter evenly among the muffin cups, filling each about two-thirds full.

Optional Parmesan Topping:
- If desired, sprinkle grated Parmesan cheese on top of each muffin.

Bake:
- Bake in the preheated oven for 18-20 minutes or until a toothpick inserted into the center comes out clean.

Cool:
- Allow the spinach and feta muffins to cool in the muffin tin for 5 minutes, then transfer them to a wire rack to cool completely.

Serve and Enjoy:
- Once cooled, serve and savor these savory spinach and feta muffins!

Tips:

- You can customize these muffins by adding ingredients like sun-dried tomatoes or black olives for extra flavor.
- If you don't have buttermilk, you can make a substitute by adding 1 tablespoon of vinegar or lemon juice to 1 cup of milk and letting it sit for 5 minutes.
- These muffins are delicious warm or at room temperature.

These savory spinach and feta muffins make for a delightful addition to brunch or a tasty savory snack. Enjoy the combination of spinach and tangy feta in every bite!

Pumpkin Spice Muffins

Ingredients:

- 1 3/4 cups all-purpose flour
- 1 teaspoon baking powder
- 1/2 teaspoon baking soda
- 1/2 teaspoon salt
- 1 teaspoon ground cinnamon
- 1/2 teaspoon ground ginger
- 1/4 teaspoon ground nutmeg
- 1/4 teaspoon ground cloves
- 1/2 cup unsalted butter, softened
- 1 cup granulated sugar
- 2 large eggs
- 1 cup canned pumpkin puree
- 1 teaspoon vanilla extract
- 1/2 cup buttermilk

Cinnamon Sugar Topping:

- 1/4 cup granulated sugar
- 1 teaspoon ground cinnamon

Instructions:

Preheat Oven:
- Preheat your oven to 375°F (190°C). Line a muffin tin with paper liners or grease the cups.

Mix Dry Ingredients:
- In a medium bowl, whisk together the flour, baking powder, baking soda, salt, cinnamon, ginger, nutmeg, and cloves.

Cream Butter and Sugar:
- In a large bowl, cream together the softened butter and granulated sugar until light and fluffy.

Add Eggs:
- Add the eggs one at a time, beating well after each addition.

Add Pumpkin and Vanilla:
- Mix in the pumpkin puree and vanilla extract until well combined.

Add Dry Ingredients:
- Gradually add the dry ingredients to the wet ingredients, alternating with the buttermilk. Begin and end with the dry ingredients, mixing until just combined. Do not overmix.

Fill Muffin Cups:
- Divide the batter evenly among the muffin cups, filling each about two-thirds full.

Prepare Cinnamon Sugar Topping:
- In a small bowl, mix together the granulated sugar and ground cinnamon for the topping.

Sprinkle Topping:
- Sprinkle the cinnamon sugar topping over the batter in each muffin cup.

Bake:
- Bake in the preheated oven for 18-20 minutes or until a toothpick inserted into the center comes out clean.

Cool:
- Allow the pumpkin spice muffins to cool in the muffin tin for 5 minutes, then transfer them to a wire rack to cool completely.

Serve and Enjoy:
- Once cooled, serve and enjoy these deliciously spiced pumpkin spice muffins!

Tips:

- For added texture and flavor, consider folding in chopped nuts or raisins into the batter.
- These muffins are perfect for fall, but they can be enjoyed year-round.
- Serve with a dollop of whipped cream or cream cheese frosting for an extra treat.

These pumpkin spice muffins capture the warm flavors of fall and are a delightful addition to your breakfast or snack repertoire. Enjoy the comforting taste of pumpkin and spices in every bite!

Almond Flour Banana Muffins

Ingredients:

- 2 cups almond flour
- 1/2 teaspoon baking soda
- 1/4 teaspoon salt
- 1/2 teaspoon ground cinnamon
- 3 ripe bananas, mashed
- 1/4 cup coconut oil, melted (or melted butter)
- 3 large eggs
- 1 teaspoon vanilla extract
- 1/4 cup honey or maple syrup
- 1/2 cup chopped nuts (walnuts or pecans), optional

Instructions:

Preheat Oven:
- Preheat your oven to 350°F (175°C). Line a muffin tin with paper liners or grease the cups.

Mix Dry Ingredients:
- In a large bowl, whisk together the almond flour, baking soda, salt, and ground cinnamon.

Combine Wet Ingredients:
- In another bowl, mix together the mashed bananas, melted coconut oil (or butter), eggs, vanilla extract, and honey (or maple syrup).

Combine Wet and Dry Ingredients:
- Add the wet ingredients to the dry ingredients, stirring until just combined. Do not overmix.

Fold in Chopped Nuts:
- If using nuts, gently fold in the chopped nuts until evenly distributed throughout the batter.

Fill Muffin Cups:
- Divide the batter evenly among the muffin cups, filling each about two-thirds full.

Bake:
- Bake in the preheated oven for 20-25 minutes or until a toothpick inserted into the center comes out clean.

Cool:

- Allow the almond flour banana muffins to cool in the muffin tin for 5 minutes, then transfer them to a wire rack to cool completely.

Serve and Enjoy:
- Once cooled, serve and enjoy these gluten-free and grain-free almond flour banana muffins!

Tips:

- Make sure to use ripe bananas for a naturally sweet flavor.
- Almond flour can vary in texture; if your batter is too thick, you can add a tablespoon or two of almond milk to achieve the desired consistency.
- These muffins are naturally sweetened, but you can adjust the sweetness by adding more or less honey or maple syrup.

These almond flour banana muffins are a delicious gluten-free option, perfect for those looking for a grain-free and wholesome treat. Enjoy them as a snack or part of a healthy breakfast!

Decadent Chocolate Cupcakes:
Classic Chocolate Cupcakes

Ingredients:

- 1 cup all-purpose flour
- 1/2 cup unsweetened cocoa powder
- 1 teaspoon baking powder
- 1/2 teaspoon baking soda
- 1/4 teaspoon salt
- 1/2 cup unsalted butter, softened
- 1 cup granulated sugar
- 2 large eggs
- 2 teaspoons vanilla extract
- 1/2 cup sour cream
- 1/2 cup whole milk

Chocolate Buttercream Frosting:

- 1 cup unsalted butter, softened
- 2 cups powdered sugar
- 1/2 cup unsweetened cocoa powder
- 1 teaspoon vanilla extract
- 2-3 tablespoons whole milk

Instructions:

Preheat Oven:
- Preheat your oven to 350°F (175°C). Line a muffin tin with cupcake liners.

Mix Dry Ingredients:
- In a medium bowl, whisk together the flour, cocoa powder, baking powder, baking soda, and salt.

Cream Butter and Sugar:
- In a large bowl, cream together the softened butter and granulated sugar until light and fluffy.

Add Eggs and Vanilla:
- Add the eggs one at a time, beating well after each addition. Stir in the vanilla extract.

Add Dry Ingredients Alternately with Wet Ingredients:

- Gradually add the dry ingredients to the wet ingredients, alternating with the sour cream and milk. Begin and end with the dry ingredients, mixing until just combined. Do not overmix.

Fill Cupcake Liners:
- Divide the batter evenly among the cupcake liners, filling each about two-thirds full.

Bake:
- Bake in the preheated oven for 18-20 minutes or until a toothpick inserted into the center comes out clean.

Cool:
- Allow the chocolate cupcakes to cool in the muffin tin for 5 minutes, then transfer them to a wire rack to cool completely.

Prepare Chocolate Buttercream Frosting:
- In a large bowl, beat together the softened butter, powdered sugar, cocoa powder, and vanilla extract. Gradually add the milk until the desired consistency is reached.

Frost Cupcakes:
- Once the cupcakes are completely cooled, frost them with the chocolate buttercream frosting.

Serve and Enjoy:
- Once frosted, serve and enjoy these classic chocolate cupcakes!

Tips:

- Make sure your ingredients, especially the butter and eggs, are at room temperature for a smoother batter.
- You can use a piping bag to create decorative swirls with the frosting.
- Top with chocolate shavings or sprinkles for extra flair.

These classic chocolate cupcakes are a crowd-pleaser and are perfect for any occasion. The combination of moist chocolate cake and rich chocolate buttercream is simply irresistible!

Double Chocolate Chip Cupcakes

Ingredients:

- 1 1/2 cups all-purpose flour
- 1/2 cup unsweetened cocoa powder
- 1 teaspoon baking powder
- 1/2 teaspoon baking soda
- 1/4 teaspoon salt
- 1/2 cup unsalted butter, softened
- 1 cup granulated sugar
- 2 large eggs
- 1 teaspoon vanilla extract
- 1/2 cup sour cream
- 1/2 cup hot water
- 1 cup semi-sweet chocolate chips

Chocolate Ganache:

- 1/2 cup heavy cream
- 1 cup semi-sweet chocolate chips

Instructions:

Preheat Oven:
- Preheat your oven to 350°F (175°C). Line a muffin tin with cupcake liners.

Mix Dry Ingredients:
- In a medium bowl, whisk together the flour, cocoa powder, baking powder, baking soda, and salt.

Cream Butter and Sugar:
- In a large bowl, cream together the softened butter and granulated sugar until light and fluffy.

Add Eggs and Vanilla:
- Add the eggs one at a time, beating well after each addition. Stir in the vanilla extract.

Add Dry Ingredients Alternately with Sour Cream and Hot Water:

- Gradually add the dry ingredients to the wet ingredients, alternating with the sour cream and hot water. Begin and end with the dry ingredients, mixing until just combined. Do not overmix.

Fold in Chocolate Chips:
- Gently fold in the chocolate chips until evenly distributed throughout the batter.

Fill Cupcake Liners:
- Divide the batter evenly among the cupcake liners, filling each about two-thirds full.

Bake:
- Bake in the preheated oven for 18-20 minutes or until a toothpick inserted into the center comes out clean.

Cool:
- Allow the double chocolate chip cupcakes to cool in the muffin tin for 5 minutes, then transfer them to a wire rack to cool completely.

Prepare Chocolate Ganache:
- In a small saucepan, heat the heavy cream over medium heat until it just begins to simmer. Remove from heat and pour over the chocolate chips in a bowl. Let it sit for a minute, then stir until smooth.

Dip or Drizzle Ganache:
- Dip the tops of the cooled cupcakes into the chocolate ganache or drizzle it over the cupcakes.

Serve and Enjoy:
- Once the ganache has set, serve and indulge in these decadent double chocolate chip cupcakes!

Tips:

- For an extra chocolatey experience, you can add a handful of chocolate chips into the batter along with the semi-sweet chocolate chips.
- Allow the ganache to cool and set before serving to achieve a glossy finish.

These double chocolate chip cupcakes are a chocolate lover's dream, combining rich chocolate cake with a luscious chocolate ganache. Enjoy the double dose of chocolate goodness!

Chocolate Peanut Butter Cupcakes

Ingredients:

Chocolate Cupcakes:

- 1 1/2 cups all-purpose flour
- 1/2 cup unsweetened cocoa powder
- 1 teaspoon baking powder
- 1/2 teaspoon baking soda
- 1/4 teaspoon salt
- 1/2 cup unsalted butter, softened
- 1 cup granulated sugar
- 2 large eggs
- 1 teaspoon vanilla extract
- 1/2 cup sour cream
- 1/2 cup hot water

Peanut Butter Frosting:

- 1 cup unsalted butter, softened
- 1 cup creamy peanut butter
- 4 cups powdered sugar
- 1/4 cup whole milk
- 1 teaspoon vanilla extract
- Pinch of salt

Chocolate Ganache (Optional):

- 1/2 cup heavy cream
- 1 cup semi-sweet chocolate chips

Instructions:

Preheat Oven:
- Preheat your oven to 350°F (175°C). Line a muffin tin with cupcake liners.

Mix Dry Ingredients for Cupcakes:
- In a medium bowl, whisk together the flour, cocoa powder, baking powder, baking soda, and salt.

Cream Butter and Sugar for Cupcakes:

- In a large bowl, cream together the softened butter and granulated sugar until light and fluffy.

Add Eggs and Vanilla for Cupcakes:
- Add the eggs one at a time, beating well after each addition. Stir in the vanilla extract.

Add Dry Ingredients Alternately with Sour Cream and Hot Water:
- Gradually add the dry ingredients to the wet ingredients, alternating with the sour cream and hot water. Begin and end with the dry ingredients, mixing until just combined. Do not overmix.

Fill Cupcake Liners:
- Divide the batter evenly among the cupcake liners, filling each about two-thirds full.

Bake Cupcakes:
- Bake in the preheated oven for 18-20 minutes or until a toothpick inserted into the center comes out clean.

Cool Cupcakes:
- Allow the chocolate cupcakes to cool in the muffin tin for 5 minutes, then transfer them to a wire rack to cool completely.

Make Peanut Butter Frosting:
- In a large bowl, beat together the softened butter and peanut butter until smooth. Gradually add the powdered sugar, milk, vanilla extract, and a pinch of salt. Beat until creamy and well combined.

Frost Cupcakes with Peanut Butter Frosting:
- Once the cupcakes are completely cooled, frost them with the peanut butter frosting.

Optional: Make Chocolate Ganache:
- In a small saucepan, heat the heavy cream over medium heat until it just begins to simmer. Remove from heat and pour over the chocolate chips in a bowl. Let it sit for a minute, then stir until smooth. Drizzle or dip the tops of the peanut butter-frosted cupcakes into the chocolate ganache.

Serve and Enjoy:
- Once frosted or ganached, serve and savor these irresistible chocolate peanut butter cupcakes!

Tips:

- For added texture, sprinkle chopped peanuts on top of the peanut butter frosting.
- If you opt for the chocolate ganache, allow it to set before serving.

These chocolate peanut butter cupcakes are a delightful combination of rich chocolate and creamy peanut butter, making them a perfect treat for those who love this classic flavor pairing!

Chocolate Mint Cupcakes

Ingredients:

Chocolate Cupcakes:

- 1 1/2 cups all-purpose flour
- 1/2 cup unsweetened cocoa powder
- 1 teaspoon baking powder
- 1/2 teaspoon baking soda
- 1/4 teaspoon salt
- 1/2 cup unsalted butter, softened
- 1 cup granulated sugar
- 2 large eggs
- 1 teaspoon vanilla extract
- 1/2 cup sour cream
- 1/2 cup hot water

Mint Chocolate Ganache:

- 1/2 cup heavy cream
- 1 1/2 cups semi-sweet chocolate chips
- 1 teaspoon mint extract

Mint Cream Cheese Frosting:

- 1/2 cup unsalted butter, softened
- 8 oz cream cheese, softened
- 4 cups powdered sugar
- 1 teaspoon mint extract
- Green food coloring (optional)

Instructions:

Preheat Oven:
- Preheat your oven to 350°F (175°C). Line a muffin tin with cupcake liners.

Mix Dry Ingredients for Cupcakes:

- In a medium bowl, whisk together the flour, cocoa powder, baking powder, baking soda, and salt.

Cream Butter and Sugar for Cupcakes:
- In a large bowl, cream together the softened butter and granulated sugar until light and fluffy.

Add Eggs and Vanilla for Cupcakes:
- Add the eggs one at a time, beating well after each addition. Stir in the vanilla extract.

Add Dry Ingredients Alternately with Sour Cream and Hot Water:
- Gradually add the dry ingredients to the wet ingredients, alternating with the sour cream and hot water. Begin and end with the dry ingredients, mixing until just combined. Do not overmix.

Fill Cupcake Liners:
- Divide the batter evenly among the cupcake liners, filling each about two-thirds full.

Bake Cupcakes:
- Bake in the preheated oven for 18-20 minutes or until a toothpick inserted into the center comes out clean.

Cool Cupcakes:
- Allow the chocolate cupcakes to cool in the muffin tin for 5 minutes, then transfer them to a wire rack to cool completely.

Make Mint Chocolate Ganache:
- In a small saucepan, heat the heavy cream over medium heat until it just begins to simmer. Remove from heat and pour over the chocolate chips in a bowl. Let it sit for a minute, then stir until smooth. Stir in the mint extract. Let the ganache cool slightly.

Dip or Drizzle Cupcakes with Mint Chocolate Ganache:
- Dip the tops of the cooled cupcakes into the mint chocolate ganache or drizzle it over the cupcakes.

Make Mint Cream Cheese Frosting:
- In a large bowl, beat together the softened butter, cream cheese, powdered sugar, mint extract, and green food coloring (if using) until smooth and creamy.

Frost Cupcakes:
- Once the ganache has set, frost the cupcakes with the mint cream cheese frosting.

Serve and Enjoy:
- Once frosted, serve and relish these delectable chocolate mint cupcakes!

Tips:

- Adjust the amount of mint extract to your preference, starting with a smaller amount and adding more if needed.
- If you prefer a stronger green color, you can use gel food coloring for the frosting.
- Garnish with chocolate shavings or mint leaves for an elegant touch.

These chocolate mint cupcakes are a delightful blend of rich chocolate, refreshing mint, and creamy frosting. Perfect for mint chocolate enthusiasts or any festive occasion!

Chocolate Espresso Cupcakes

Ingredients:

Chocolate Espresso Cupcakes:

- 1 1/2 cups all-purpose flour
- 1/2 cup unsweetened cocoa powder
- 1 teaspoon baking powder
- 1/2 teaspoon baking soda
- 1/4 teaspoon salt
- 1/2 cup unsalted butter, softened
- 1 cup granulated sugar
- 2 large eggs
- 1 teaspoon vanilla extract
- 1/2 cup sour cream
- 1/2 cup strong brewed espresso, cooled

Espresso Chocolate Ganache:

- 1/2 cup heavy cream
- 1 1/2 cups semi-sweet chocolate chips
- 2 tablespoons strong brewed espresso

Espresso Buttercream Frosting:

- 1 cup unsalted butter, softened
- 3 cups powdered sugar
- 2 tablespoons strong brewed espresso
- 1 teaspoon vanilla extract
- Chocolate-covered coffee beans for garnish (optional)

Instructions:

Preheat Oven:
- Preheat your oven to 350°F (175°C). Line a muffin tin with cupcake liners.

Mix Dry Ingredients for Cupcakes:

- In a medium bowl, whisk together the flour, cocoa powder, baking powder, baking soda, and salt.

Cream Butter and Sugar for Cupcakes:
- In a large bowl, cream together the softened butter and granulated sugar until light and fluffy.

Add Eggs and Vanilla for Cupcakes:
- Add the eggs one at a time, beating well after each addition. Stir in the vanilla extract.

Add Dry Ingredients Alternately with Sour Cream and Espresso:
- Gradually add the dry ingredients to the wet ingredients, alternating with the sour cream and espresso. Begin and end with the dry ingredients, mixing until just combined. Do not overmix.

Fill Cupcake Liners:
- Divide the batter evenly among the cupcake liners, filling each about two-thirds full.

Bake Cupcakes:
- Bake in the preheated oven for 18-20 minutes or until a toothpick inserted into the center comes out clean.

Cool Cupcakes:
- Allow the chocolate espresso cupcakes to cool in the muffin tin for 5 minutes, then transfer them to a wire rack to cool completely.

Make Espresso Chocolate Ganache:
- In a small saucepan, heat the heavy cream over medium heat until it just begins to simmer. Remove from heat and pour over the chocolate chips in a bowl. Let it sit for a minute, then stir until smooth. Stir in the brewed espresso. Let the ganache cool slightly.

Dip or Drizzle Cupcakes with Espresso Chocolate Ganache:
- Dip the tops of the cooled cupcakes into the espresso chocolate ganache or drizzle it over the cupcakes.

Make Espresso Buttercream Frosting:
- In a large bowl, beat together the softened butter, powdered sugar, brewed espresso, and vanilla extract until smooth and creamy.

Frost Cupcakes:
- Once the ganache has set, frost the cupcakes with the espresso buttercream frosting.

Garnish and Serve:
- If desired, garnish with chocolate-covered coffee beans.

Serve and Enjoy:

- Once frosted and garnished, serve and enjoy these delightful chocolate espresso cupcakes!

Tips:

- Adjust the strength of the espresso in both the cupcakes and the ganache according to your preference.
- For an extra coffee kick, you can add a teaspoon of instant espresso powder to the cupcake batter.
- Use a piping bag to pipe the espresso buttercream frosting for a polished look.

These chocolate espresso cupcakes are a perfect blend of rich chocolate and bold coffee flavors. They are a delightful treat for coffee lovers and a great addition to any special occasion!

Dark Chocolate Raspberry Cupcakes

Ingredients:

Dark Chocolate Raspberry Cupcakes:

- 1 1/2 cups all-purpose flour
- 1/2 cup unsweetened cocoa powder
- 1 teaspoon baking powder
- 1/2 teaspoon baking soda
- 1/4 teaspoon salt
- 1/2 cup unsalted butter, softened
- 1 cup granulated sugar
- 2 large eggs
- 1 teaspoon vanilla extract
- 1/2 cup sour cream
- 1/2 cup buttermilk
- 1/2 cup dark chocolate, melted and cooled
- 1 cup fresh raspberries

Raspberry Cream Cheese Frosting:

- 1/2 cup unsalted butter, softened
- 8 oz cream cheese, softened
- 4 cups powdered sugar
- 1/2 cup fresh raspberries, mashed
- 1 teaspoon vanilla extract

Instructions:

Preheat Oven:
- Preheat your oven to 350°F (175°C). Line a muffin tin with cupcake liners.

Mix Dry Ingredients for Cupcakes:
- In a medium bowl, whisk together the flour, cocoa powder, baking powder, baking soda, and salt.

Cream Butter and Sugar for Cupcakes:

- In a large bowl, cream together the softened butter and granulated sugar until light and fluffy.

Add Eggs and Vanilla for Cupcakes:
- Add the eggs one at a time, beating well after each addition. Stir in the vanilla extract.

Add Dry Ingredients Alternately with Sour Cream, Buttermilk, and Melted Chocolate:
- Gradually add the dry ingredients to the wet ingredients, alternating with the sour cream, buttermilk, and melted chocolate. Begin and end with the dry ingredients, mixing until just combined. Do not overmix.

Fold in Raspberries:
- Gently fold in the fresh raspberries until evenly distributed throughout the batter.

Fill Cupcake Liners:
- Divide the batter evenly among the cupcake liners, filling each about two-thirds full.

Bake Cupcakes:
- Bake in the preheated oven for 18-20 minutes or until a toothpick inserted into the center comes out clean.

Cool Cupcakes:
- Allow the dark chocolate raspberry cupcakes to cool in the muffin tin for 5 minutes, then transfer them to a wire rack to cool completely.

Make Raspberry Cream Cheese Frosting:
- In a large bowl, beat together the softened butter, cream cheese, powdered sugar, mashed raspberries, and vanilla extract until smooth and creamy.

Frost Cupcakes:
- Once the cupcakes are completely cooled, frost them with the raspberry cream cheese frosting.

Serve and Enjoy:
- Once frosted, serve and enjoy these decadent dark chocolate raspberry cupcakes!

Tips:

- Ensure the melted dark chocolate has cooled to room temperature before adding it to the batter.
- For a smoother frosting, you can strain the mashed raspberries to remove seeds before adding them to the cream cheese frosting.

- Garnish with additional fresh raspberries for a beautiful presentation.

These dark chocolate raspberry cupcakes are a delightful combination of rich chocolate and the tartness of fresh raspberries. They make for an elegant and delicious treat for any occasion!

Fruity Cupcakes:
Strawberry Cupcakes

Ingredients:

Strawberry Cupcakes:

- 1 1/2 cups all-purpose flour
- 1 1/2 teaspoons baking powder
- 1/4 teaspoon salt
- 1/2 cup unsalted butter, softened
- 1 cup granulated sugar
- 2 large eggs
- 1 teaspoon vanilla extract
- 1/2 cup whole milk
- 1 cup fresh strawberries, finely chopped

Strawberry Cream Cheese Frosting:

- 1/2 cup unsalted butter, softened
- 8 oz cream cheese, softened
- 4 cups powdered sugar
- 1/2 cup fresh strawberries, pureed
- 1 teaspoon vanilla extract

Instructions:

Preheat Oven:
- Preheat your oven to 350°F (175°C). Line a muffin tin with cupcake liners.

Mix Dry Ingredients for Cupcakes:
- In a medium bowl, whisk together the flour, baking powder, and salt.

Cream Butter and Sugar for Cupcakes:
- In a large bowl, cream together the softened butter and granulated sugar until light and fluffy.

Add Eggs and Vanilla for Cupcakes:
- Add the eggs one at a time, beating well after each addition. Stir in the vanilla extract.

Add Dry Ingredients Alternately with Milk:

- Gradually add the dry ingredients to the wet ingredients, alternating with the whole milk. Begin and end with the dry ingredients, mixing until just combined. Do not overmix.

Fold in Chopped Strawberries:
- Gently fold in the finely chopped fresh strawberries until evenly distributed throughout the batter.

Fill Cupcake Liners:
- Divide the batter evenly among the cupcake liners, filling each about two-thirds full.

Bake Cupcakes:
- Bake in the preheated oven for 18-20 minutes or until a toothpick inserted into the center comes out clean.

Cool Cupcakes:
- Allow the strawberry cupcakes to cool in the muffin tin for 5 minutes, then transfer them to a wire rack to cool completely.

Make Strawberry Cream Cheese Frosting:
- In a large bowl, beat together the softened butter, cream cheese, powdered sugar, strawberry puree, and vanilla extract until smooth and creamy.

Frost Cupcakes:
- Once the cupcakes are completely cooled, frost them with the strawberry cream cheese frosting.

Serve and Enjoy:
- Once frosted, serve and savor these delicious strawberry cupcakes!

Tips:

- Ensure the fresh strawberries are ripe and sweet for the best flavor.
- Adjust the amount of strawberry puree in the frosting to achieve the desired level of strawberry flavor.
- If the frosting is too soft, you can refrigerate it for a short time to firm it up before frosting the cupcakes.

These strawberry cupcakes are a delightful and fruity treat, perfect for celebrating special occasions or satisfying your sweet cravings. Enjoy the burst of strawberry flavor in every bite!

Raspberry Lemonade Cupcakes

Ingredients:

Raspberry Lemonade Cupcakes:

- 1 1/2 cups all-purpose flour
- 1 1/2 teaspoons baking powder
- 1/4 teaspoon salt
- 1/2 cup unsalted butter, softened
- 1 cup granulated sugar
- 2 large eggs
- 1 teaspoon vanilla extract
- 1/2 cup whole milk
- Zest of 2 lemons
- 2 tablespoons fresh lemon juice
- 1/2 cup fresh raspberries, finely chopped

Raspberry Lemonade Buttercream Frosting:

- 1 cup unsalted butter, softened
- 4 cups powdered sugar
- Zest of 1 lemon
- 3 tablespoons fresh lemon juice
- 1/4 cup raspberry puree (strained)

Instructions:

Preheat Oven:
- Preheat your oven to 350°F (175°C). Line a muffin tin with cupcake liners.

Mix Dry Ingredients for Cupcakes:
- In a medium bowl, whisk together the flour, baking powder, and salt.

Cream Butter and Sugar for Cupcakes:
- In a large bowl, cream together the softened butter and granulated sugar until light and fluffy.

Add Eggs and Vanilla for Cupcakes:

- Add the eggs one at a time, beating well after each addition. Stir in the vanilla extract.

Add Dry Ingredients Alternately with Milk, Lemon Zest, and Lemon Juice:
- Gradually add the dry ingredients to the wet ingredients, alternating with the whole milk. Begin and end with the dry ingredients. Mix in the lemon zest and fresh lemon juice until just combined. Do not overmix.

Fold in Chopped Raspberries:
- Gently fold in the finely chopped fresh raspberries until evenly distributed throughout the batter.

Fill Cupcake Liners:
- Divide the batter evenly among the cupcake liners, filling each about two-thirds full.

Bake Cupcakes:
- Bake in the preheated oven for 18-20 minutes or until a toothpick inserted into the center comes out clean.

Cool Cupcakes:
- Allow the raspberry lemonade cupcakes to cool in the muffin tin for 5 minutes, then transfer them to a wire rack to cool completely.

Make Raspberry Lemonade Buttercream Frosting:
- In a large bowl, beat together the softened butter, powdered sugar, lemon zest, lemon juice, and raspberry puree until smooth and creamy.

Frost Cupcakes:
- Once the cupcakes are completely cooled, frost them with the raspberry lemonade buttercream frosting.

Garnish and Serve:
- Garnish with additional lemon zest or a fresh raspberry on top if desired.

Serve and Enjoy:
- Once frosted and garnished, serve and enjoy these refreshing raspberry lemonade cupcakes!

Tips:

- Make sure the raspberries are fresh and ripe for the best flavor.
- If the raspberry puree is too thick, you can add a little water to achieve a smooth consistency.
- Adjust the amount of lemon juice in the frosting to balance the sweetness according to your taste.

These raspberry lemonade cupcakes are a delightful combination of tangy lemon and sweet raspberries, making them a perfect treat for warm days or any occasion. Enjoy the burst of fruity flavors!

Mango Coconut Cupcakes

Ingredients:

Mango Coconut Cupcakes:

- 1 1/2 cups all-purpose flour
- 1 1/2 teaspoons baking powder
- 1/4 teaspoon salt
- 1/2 cup unsalted butter, softened
- 1 cup granulated sugar
- 2 large eggs
- 1 teaspoon vanilla extract
- 1/2 cup coconut milk
- 1/2 cup mango puree (fresh or canned)
- 1/2 cup shredded coconut (sweetened or unsweetened)

Coconut Cream Cheese Frosting:

- 1/2 cup unsalted butter, softened
- 8 oz cream cheese, softened
- 4 cups powdered sugar
- 1/2 cup shredded coconut (for decoration)

Instructions:

Preheat Oven:
- Preheat your oven to 350°F (175°C). Line a muffin tin with cupcake liners.

Mix Dry Ingredients for Cupcakes:
- In a medium bowl, whisk together the flour, baking powder, and salt.

Cream Butter and Sugar for Cupcakes:
- In a large bowl, cream together the softened butter and granulated sugar until light and fluffy.

Add Eggs and Vanilla for Cupcakes:
- Add the eggs one at a time, beating well after each addition. Stir in the vanilla extract.

Add Dry Ingredients Alternately with Coconut Milk and Mango Puree:

- Gradually add the dry ingredients to the wet ingredients, alternating with the coconut milk and mango puree. Begin and end with the dry ingredients, mixing until just combined. Do not overmix.

Fold in Shredded Coconut:
- Gently fold in the shredded coconut until evenly distributed throughout the batter.

Fill Cupcake Liners:
- Divide the batter evenly among the cupcake liners, filling each about two-thirds full.

Bake Cupcakes:
- Bake in the preheated oven for 18-20 minutes or until a toothpick inserted into the center comes out clean.

Cool Cupcakes:
- Allow the mango coconut cupcakes to cool in the muffin tin for 5 minutes, then transfer them to a wire rack to cool completely.

Make Coconut Cream Cheese Frosting:
- In a large bowl, beat together the softened butter, cream cheese, powdered sugar, and shredded coconut until smooth and creamy.

Frost Cupcakes:
- Once the cupcakes are completely cooled, frost them with the coconut cream cheese frosting.

Garnish and Serve:
- Garnish with additional shredded coconut on top for decoration.

Serve and Enjoy:
- Once frosted and garnished, serve and savor these tropical-inspired mango coconut cupcakes!

Tips:

- If using sweetened shredded coconut, adjust the sugar in the cupcake batter and frosting accordingly.
- Ensure the mango puree is smooth and has a sweet flavor.
- Toast the shredded coconut for a few minutes in a dry skillet for added flavor before using it as a garnish.

These mango coconut cupcakes offer a delightful combination of tropical flavors. They are perfect for summer gatherings, celebrations, or whenever you're in the mood for a sweet and exotic treat!

Pineapple Upside-Down Cupcakes

Ingredients:

Pineapple Upside-Down Topping:

- 1/4 cup unsalted butter
- 1/2 cup brown sugar, packed
- 1 can (20 oz) pineapple slices, drained
- Maraschino cherries (one for each cupcake)

Cupcake Batter:

- 1 1/2 cups all-purpose flour
- 1 1/2 teaspoons baking powder
- 1/4 teaspoon salt
- 1/2 cup unsalted butter, softened
- 1 cup granulated sugar
- 2 large eggs
- 1 teaspoon vanilla extract
- 1/2 cup pineapple juice (reserved from the canned pineapple)
- 1/2 cup buttermilk

Instructions:

Preheat Oven:
- Preheat your oven to 350°F (175°C). Line a muffin tin with cupcake liners.

Prepare Pineapple Upside-Down Topping:
- In a saucepan over medium heat, melt the butter. Add the brown sugar and stir until it dissolves and becomes a caramel-like consistency.
- Spoon a tablespoon of the brown sugar mixture into each cupcake liner.
- Place a pineapple slice in each cup and top with a maraschino cherry in the center.

Mix Dry Ingredients for Cupcakes:
- In a medium bowl, whisk together the flour, baking powder, and salt.

Cream Butter and Sugar for Cupcakes:

- In a large bowl, cream together the softened butter and granulated sugar until light and fluffy.

Add Eggs and Vanilla for Cupcakes:
- Add the eggs one at a time, beating well after each addition. Stir in the vanilla extract.

Combine Dry Ingredients with Pineapple Juice and Buttermilk:
- Gradually add the dry ingredients to the wet ingredients, alternating with the pineapple juice and buttermilk. Begin and end with the dry ingredients, mixing until just combined. Do not overmix.

Fill Cupcake Liners:
- Divide the batter evenly among the cupcake liners, placing it on top of the pineapple slice and brown sugar mixture.

Bake Cupcakes:
- Bake in the preheated oven for 18-20 minutes or until a toothpick inserted into the center comes out clean.

Cool Cupcakes:
- Allow the pineapple upside-down cupcakes to cool in the muffin tin for 5 minutes, then transfer them to a wire rack to cool completely.

Serve and Enjoy:
- Once cooled, serve these delightful pineapple upside-down cupcakes with the pineapple and cherry side facing up!

Tips:

- Ensure the brown sugar mixture has a caramel-like consistency before spooning it into the cupcake liners.
- Use pineapple juice reserved from the canned pineapple for the best flavor in the cupcake batter.
- You can substitute buttermilk with regular milk mixed with a teaspoon of white vinegar or lemon juice if needed.

These pineapple upside-down cupcakes capture the classic flavors of the traditional cake but in individual servings. They are a delightful and nostalgic treat for any occasion!

Peach Cobbler Cupcakes

Ingredients:

Peach Filling:

- 2 cups fresh or canned peaches, peeled and diced
- 1/3 cup granulated sugar
- 1 tablespoon lemon juice
- 1 tablespoon cornstarch
- 1/2 teaspoon ground cinnamon
- Pinch of nutmeg

Cupcake Batter:

- 1 1/2 cups all-purpose flour
- 1 1/2 teaspoons baking powder
- 1/4 teaspoon salt
- 1/2 cup unsalted butter, softened
- 1 cup granulated sugar
- 2 large eggs
- 1 teaspoon vanilla extract
- 1/2 cup buttermilk

Crumble Topping:

- 1/3 cup all-purpose flour
- 1/3 cup brown sugar, packed
- 1/4 cup unsalted butter, melted
- 1/2 teaspoon ground cinnamon
- Pinch of salt

Vanilla Glaze:

- 1 cup powdered sugar
- 2 tablespoons milk
- 1/2 teaspoon vanilla extract

Instructions:

Preheat Oven:
- Preheat your oven to 350°F (175°C). Line a muffin tin with cupcake liners.

Prepare Peach Filling:
- In a saucepan over medium heat, combine diced peaches, granulated sugar, lemon juice, cornstarch, cinnamon, and nutmeg. Cook until the mixture thickens, stirring occasionally. Remove from heat and set aside to cool.

Mix Dry Ingredients for Cupcakes:
- In a medium bowl, whisk together the flour, baking powder, and salt.

Cream Butter and Sugar for Cupcakes:
- In a large bowl, cream together the softened butter and granulated sugar until light and fluffy.

Add Eggs and Vanilla for Cupcakes:
- Add the eggs one at a time, beating well after each addition. Stir in the vanilla extract.

Combine Dry Ingredients with Buttermilk:
- Gradually add the dry ingredients to the wet ingredients, alternating with the buttermilk. Begin and end with the dry ingredients, mixing until just combined. Do not overmix.

Fill Cupcake Liners:
- Divide the batter evenly among the cupcake liners, filling each about two-thirds full.

Add Peach Filling and Crumble Topping:
- Spoon a tablespoon of the peach filling on top of the cupcake batter.
- In a small bowl, combine the crumble topping ingredients (flour, brown sugar, melted butter, cinnamon, and salt). Sprinkle the crumble topping over the peach filling.

Bake Cupcakes:
- Bake in the preheated oven for 18-20 minutes or until a toothpick inserted into the center comes out clean.

Make Vanilla Glaze:
- In a bowl, whisk together powdered sugar, milk, and vanilla extract until smooth.

Glaze and Serve:
- Once the cupcakes are cooled, drizzle them with the vanilla glaze.

Serve and Enjoy:
- Serve these peach cobbler cupcakes and savor the delightful combination of flavors!

Tips:

- Adjust the sugar in the peach filling according to the sweetness of your peaches.
- Ensure the crumble topping is evenly distributed for a crunchy texture.
- Drizzle the glaze over the cupcakes just before serving for a fresh and glossy finish.

These peach cobbler cupcakes capture the essence of a classic Southern dessert in a delightful handheld treat. Enjoy the warmth of peach filling, the crumbly topping, and the sweet vanilla glaze in every bite!

Blackberry Vanilla Cupcakes

Ingredients:

Blackberry Vanilla Cupcakes:

- 1 1/2 cups all-purpose flour
- 1 1/2 teaspoons baking powder
- 1/4 teaspoon salt
- 1/2 cup unsalted butter, softened
- 1 cup granulated sugar
- 2 large eggs
- 1 teaspoon vanilla extract
- 1/2 cup whole milk
- 1 cup fresh blackberries, pureed

Blackberry Vanilla Buttercream Frosting:

- 1 cup unsalted butter, softened
- 4 cups powdered sugar
- 1/4 cup blackberry puree
- 1 teaspoon vanilla extract

Instructions:

Preheat Oven:
- Preheat your oven to 350°F (175°C). Line a muffin tin with cupcake liners.

Mix Dry Ingredients for Cupcakes:
- In a medium bowl, whisk together the flour, baking powder, and salt.

Cream Butter and Sugar for Cupcakes:
- In a large bowl, cream together the softened butter and granulated sugar until light and fluffy.

Add Eggs and Vanilla for Cupcakes:
- Add the eggs one at a time, beating well after each addition. Stir in the vanilla extract.

Combine Dry Ingredients Alternately with Milk and Blackberry Puree:
- Gradually add the dry ingredients to the wet ingredients, alternating with the whole milk and blackberry puree. Begin and end with the dry ingredients, mixing until just combined. Do not overmix.

Fill Cupcake Liners:
- Divide the batter evenly among the cupcake liners, filling each about two-thirds full.

Bake Cupcakes:
- Bake in the preheated oven for 18-20 minutes or until a toothpick inserted into the center comes out clean.

Cool Cupcakes:
- Allow the blackberry vanilla cupcakes to cool in the muffin tin for 5 minutes, then transfer them to a wire rack to cool completely.

Make Blackberry Vanilla Buttercream Frosting:
- In a large bowl, beat together the softened butter, powdered sugar, blackberry puree, and vanilla extract until smooth and creamy.

Frost Cupcakes:
- Once the cupcakes are completely cooled, frost them with the blackberry vanilla buttercream frosting.

Garnish and Serve:
- Garnish with a fresh blackberry on top for decoration.

Serve and Enjoy:
- Once frosted and garnished, serve and enjoy these luscious blackberry vanilla cupcakes!

Tips:

- Ensure the blackberries are pureed into a smooth consistency for both the cupcake batter and the frosting.
- Adjust the amount of blackberry puree in the frosting to achieve the desired level of blackberry flavor.
- If the frosting is too soft, you can refrigerate it for a short time to firm it up before frosting the cupcakes.

These blackberry vanilla cupcakes offer a burst of fruity flavor and a touch of elegance. They are perfect for special occasions, celebrations, or whenever you crave a delightful and unique cupcake experience!

Gourmet Flavors:
Salted Caramel Cupcakes

Ingredients:

Cupcakes:

- 1 1/2 cups all-purpose flour
- 1 1/2 teaspoons baking powder
- 1/4 teaspoon salt
- 1/2 cup unsalted butter, softened
- 1 cup granulated sugar
- 2 large eggs
- 1 teaspoon vanilla extract
- 1/2 cup whole milk

Salted Caramel Sauce:

- 1 cup granulated sugar
- 6 tablespoons unsalted butter, cut into pieces
- 1/2 cup heavy cream
- 1 teaspoon sea salt (adjust to taste)

Salted Caramel Buttercream Frosting:

- 1 cup unsalted butter, softened
- 4 cups powdered sugar
- 1/2 cup salted caramel sauce (cooled)
- 1 teaspoon vanilla extract
- Sea salt for sprinkling (optional)

Instructions:

Preheat Oven:
- Preheat your oven to 350°F (175°C). Line a muffin tin with cupcake liners.

Mix Dry Ingredients for Cupcakes:
- In a medium bowl, whisk together the flour, baking powder, and salt.

Cream Butter and Sugar for Cupcakes:
- In a large bowl, cream together the softened butter and granulated sugar until light and fluffy.

Add Eggs and Vanilla for Cupcakes:
- Add the eggs one at a time, beating well after each addition. Stir in the vanilla extract.

Combine Dry Ingredients Alternately with Milk:
- Gradually add the dry ingredients to the wet ingredients, alternating with the whole milk. Begin and end with the dry ingredients, mixing until just combined. Do not overmix.

Fill Cupcake Liners:
- Divide the batter evenly among the cupcake liners, filling each about two-thirds full.

Bake Cupcakes:
- Bake in the preheated oven for 18-20 minutes or until a toothpick inserted into the center comes out clean.

Cool Cupcakes:
- Allow the cupcakes to cool in the muffin tin for 5 minutes, then transfer them to a wire rack to cool completely.

Make Salted Caramel Sauce:
- In a saucepan over medium heat, melt the granulated sugar until it turns amber in color. Add the butter and stir until melted. Slowly add the heavy cream while continuously stirring. Remove from heat and stir in the sea salt. Set aside to cool.

Make Salted Caramel Buttercream Frosting:
- In a large bowl, beat together the softened butter, powdered sugar, salted caramel sauce, and vanilla extract until smooth and creamy.

Frost Cupcakes:
- Once the cupcakes are completely cooled, frost them with the salted caramel buttercream frosting.

Drizzle with Salted Caramel Sauce:
- Drizzle each cupcake with a little extra salted caramel sauce.

Sprinkle with Sea Salt (Optional):
- If desired, sprinkle a small pinch of sea salt on top of each cupcake for an extra burst of saltiness.

Serve and Enjoy:
- Once frosted and drizzled, serve and savor these indulgent salted caramel cupcakes!

Tips:

- Be careful when making the salted caramel sauce, as melted sugar can be very hot. Handle it with caution.
- Adjust the amount of sea salt in the caramel sauce and the frosting to suit your taste preferences.
- Drizzling additional caramel sauce on top of the cupcakes enhances the flavor and adds a beautiful finishing touch.

These salted caramel cupcakes offer a perfect balance of sweetness and saltiness, making them a decadent treat for any occasion. Enjoy the rich caramel flavor in every bite!

Red Velvet Cupcakes

Ingredients:

Red Velvet Cupcakes:

- 1 1/2 cups all-purpose flour
- 1 cup granulated sugar
- 1/2 teaspoon baking powder
- 1/2 teaspoon baking soda
- 1/4 teaspoon salt
- 2 tablespoons cocoa powder
- 3/4 cup vegetable oil
- 2/3 cup buttermilk, room temperature
- 2 large eggs, room temperature
- 2 tablespoons red food coloring
- 1 teaspoon vanilla extract
- 1 teaspoon white vinegar or apple cider vinegar

Cream Cheese Frosting:

- 8 oz cream cheese, softened
- 1/2 cup unsalted butter, softened
- 4 cups powdered sugar
- 1 teaspoon vanilla extract

Instructions:

Preheat Oven:
- Preheat your oven to 350°F (175°C). Line a muffin tin with cupcake liners.

Mix Dry Ingredients for Cupcakes:
- In a medium bowl, whisk together the flour, sugar, baking powder, baking soda, salt, and cocoa powder.

Combine Wet Ingredients:
- In a separate large bowl, whisk together the vegetable oil, buttermilk, eggs, red food coloring, vanilla extract, and vinegar.

Combine Dry and Wet Ingredients:

- Gradually add the dry ingredients to the wet ingredients, mixing until just combined. Do not overmix.

Fill Cupcake Liners:
- Divide the batter evenly among the cupcake liners, filling each about two-thirds full.

Bake Cupcakes:
- Bake in the preheated oven for 18-20 minutes or until a toothpick inserted into the center comes out clean.

Cool Cupcakes:
- Allow the red velvet cupcakes to cool in the muffin tin for 5 minutes, then transfer them to a wire rack to cool completely.

Make Cream Cheese Frosting:
- In a large bowl, beat together the softened cream cheese, softened butter, powdered sugar, and vanilla extract until smooth and creamy.

Frost Cupcakes:
- Once the cupcakes are completely cooled, frost them with the cream cheese frosting.

Garnish (Optional):
- Optionally, garnish with red velvet cake crumbs or sprinkles for decoration.

Serve and Enjoy:
- Once frosted and garnished, serve and enjoy these classic red velvet cupcakes!

Tips:

- Use gel food coloring for a more vibrant red color in the cupcakes.
- Ensure the buttermilk, eggs, and butter are at room temperature for a smoother batter and frosting.
- If you don't have buttermilk, you can make a substitute by adding 1 tablespoon of white vinegar or lemon juice to 2/3 cup of milk and letting it sit for a few minutes.

These red velvet cupcakes are a timeless and beloved dessert. With their rich color and delicious cream cheese frosting, they make a perfect treat for special occasions or any time you're craving a classic and decadent cupcake. Enjoy!

Pistachio Cupcakes

Ingredients:

Pistachio Cupcakes:

- 1 1/2 cups all-purpose flour
- 1 1/2 teaspoons baking powder
- 1/4 teaspoon salt
- 1/2 cup unsalted butter, softened
- 1 cup granulated sugar
- 2 large eggs
- 1 teaspoon vanilla extract
- 1/2 cup pistachio paste (made from ground pistachios)
- 1/2 cup whole milk

Pistachio Cream Cheese Frosting:

- 8 oz cream cheese, softened
- 1/2 cup unsalted butter, softened
- 3 cups powdered sugar
- 1/2 cup pistachio paste
- Chopped pistachios for garnish (optional)

Instructions:

Preheat Oven:
- Preheat your oven to 350°F (175°C). Line a muffin tin with cupcake liners.

Mix Dry Ingredients for Cupcakes:
- In a medium bowl, whisk together the flour, baking powder, and salt.

Cream Butter and Sugar for Cupcakes:
- In a large bowl, cream together the softened butter and granulated sugar until light and fluffy.

Add Eggs and Vanilla for Cupcakes:
- Add the eggs one at a time, beating well after each addition. Stir in the vanilla extract.

Add Pistachio Paste and Milk:

- Mix in the pistachio paste until well combined. Gradually add the dry ingredients to the wet ingredients, alternating with the milk. Begin and end with the dry ingredients, mixing until just combined. Do not overmix.

Fill Cupcake Liners:
- Divide the batter evenly among the cupcake liners, filling each about two-thirds full.

Bake Cupcakes:
- Bake in the preheated oven for 18-20 minutes or until a toothpick inserted into the center comes out clean.

Cool Cupcakes:
- Allow the pistachio cupcakes to cool in the muffin tin for 5 minutes, then transfer them to a wire rack to cool completely.

Make Pistachio Cream Cheese Frosting:
- In a large bowl, beat together the softened cream cheese, softened butter, powdered sugar, and pistachio paste until smooth and creamy.

Frost Cupcakes:
- Once the cupcakes are completely cooled, frost them with the pistachio cream cheese frosting.

Garnish (Optional):
- Optionally, garnish with chopped pistachios on top for added texture and flavor.

Serve and Enjoy:
- Once frosted and garnished, serve and savor these delightful pistachio cupcakes!

Tips:

- Make pistachio paste by grinding shelled pistachios in a food processor until smooth. You can add a little vegetable oil if needed to achieve a paste-like consistency.
- Adjust the amount of pistachio paste in the frosting to your taste preference.
- To enhance the pistachio flavor, you can add a drop or two of almond extract to the cupcake batter.

These pistachio cupcakes are a unique and flavorful treat that captures the nutty essence of pistachios. They're perfect for special occasions or whenever you want to indulge in a distinctive cupcake experience. Enjoy!

Lavender Honey Cupcakes

Ingredients:

Lavender Honey Cupcakes:

- 1 1/2 cups all-purpose flour
- 1 1/2 teaspoons baking powder
- 1/4 teaspoon salt
- 1/2 cup unsalted butter, softened
- 1 cup granulated sugar
- 2 large eggs
- 1 teaspoon vanilla extract
- 1/2 cup honey
- 1/2 cup milk
- 2 tablespoons dried culinary lavender, finely ground

Honey Lavender Buttercream Frosting:

- 1 cup unsalted butter, softened
- 4 cups powdered sugar
- 2 tablespoons honey
- 1 teaspoon vanilla extract
- 1 teaspoon dried culinary lavender, finely ground (for garnish, optional)

Instructions:

Preheat Oven:
- Preheat your oven to 350°F (175°C). Line a muffin tin with cupcake liners.

Mix Dry Ingredients for Cupcakes:
- In a medium bowl, whisk together the flour, baking powder, and salt.

Cream Butter and Sugar for Cupcakes:
- In a large bowl, cream together the softened butter and granulated sugar until light and fluffy.

Add Eggs and Vanilla for Cupcakes:
- Add the eggs one at a time, beating well after each addition. Stir in the vanilla extract.

Combine Dry Ingredients Alternately with Honey and Milk:
- Gradually add the dry ingredients to the wet ingredients, alternating with the honey and milk. Begin and end with the dry ingredients, mixing until just combined. Do not overmix.

Fold in Ground Lavender:
- Gently fold in the finely ground dried lavender until evenly distributed throughout the batter.

Fill Cupcake Liners:
- Divide the batter evenly among the cupcake liners, filling each about two-thirds full.

Bake Cupcakes:
- Bake in the preheated oven for 18-20 minutes or until a toothpick inserted into the center comes out clean.

Cool Cupcakes:
- Allow the lavender honey cupcakes to cool in the muffin tin for 5 minutes, then transfer them to a wire rack to cool completely.

Make Honey Lavender Buttercream Frosting:
- In a large bowl, beat together the softened butter, powdered sugar, honey, and vanilla extract until smooth and creamy.

Frost Cupcakes:
- Once the cupcakes are completely cooled, frost them with the honey lavender buttercream frosting.

Garnish (Optional):
- Optionally, sprinkle a pinch of finely ground dried lavender on top of each cupcake for a decorative touch and added flavor.

Serve and Enjoy:
- Once frosted and garnished, serve and savor these elegant lavender honey cupcakes!

Tips:

- Ensure the dried culinary lavender is finely ground to avoid a gritty texture in the cupcakes.
- Adjust the amount of honey and lavender in the frosting to your taste preference.
- Decorate with fresh lavender sprigs for a visually appealing presentation.

These lavender honey cupcakes offer a delicate floral flavor and a touch of sweetness. They are a sophisticated choice for special occasions or tea time. Enjoy the unique combination of lavender and honey in every bite!

Matcha Green Tea Cupcakes

Ingredients:

Matcha Green Tea Cupcakes:

- 1 1/2 cups all-purpose flour
- 1 1/2 teaspoons matcha green tea powder
- 1 teaspoon baking powder
- 1/4 teaspoon salt
- 1/2 cup unsalted butter, softened
- 1 cup granulated sugar
- 2 large eggs
- 1 teaspoon vanilla extract
- 1/2 cup whole milk

Matcha Green Tea Cream Cheese Frosting:

- 8 oz cream cheese, softened
- 1/2 cup unsalted butter, softened
- 4 cups powdered sugar
- 1 1/2 teaspoons matcha green tea powder
- 1 teaspoon vanilla extract

Instructions:

Preheat Oven:
- Preheat your oven to 350°F (175°C). Line a muffin tin with cupcake liners.

Mix Dry Ingredients for Cupcakes:
- In a medium bowl, whisk together the flour, matcha green tea powder, baking powder, and salt.

Cream Butter and Sugar for Cupcakes:
- In a large bowl, cream together the softened butter and granulated sugar until light and fluffy.

Add Eggs and Vanilla for Cupcakes:
- Add the eggs one at a time, beating well after each addition. Stir in the vanilla extract.

Combine Dry Ingredients Alternately with Milk:

- Gradually add the dry ingredients to the wet ingredients, alternating with the whole milk. Begin and end with the dry ingredients, mixing until just combined. Do not overmix.

Fill Cupcake Liners:
- Divide the batter evenly among the cupcake liners, filling each about two-thirds full.

Bake Cupcakes:
- Bake in the preheated oven for 18-20 minutes or until a toothpick inserted into the center comes out clean.

Cool Cupcakes:
- Allow the matcha green tea cupcakes to cool in the muffin tin for 5 minutes, then transfer them to a wire rack to cool completely.

Make Matcha Green Tea Cream Cheese Frosting:
- In a large bowl, beat together the softened cream cheese, softened butter, powdered sugar, matcha green tea powder, and vanilla extract until smooth and creamy.

Frost Cupcakes:
- Once the cupcakes are completely cooled, frost them with the matcha green tea cream cheese frosting.

Garnish (Optional):
- Optionally, garnish with a sprinkle of matcha green tea powder or edible flowers for a decorative touch.

Serve and Enjoy:
- Once frosted and garnished, serve and enjoy these unique and flavorful matcha green tea cupcakes!

Tips:

- Choose high-quality matcha green tea powder for a vibrant color and rich flavor.
- Adjust the amount of matcha powder in the frosting to your taste preference.
- For a smoother frosting, ensure that the cream cheese and butter are at room temperature.

These matcha green tea cupcakes offer a delightful combination of earthy and sweet flavors. They are a perfect choice for those who appreciate the unique taste of matcha. Enjoy the distinct green tea essence in every bite!

Earl Grey Cupcakes with Lemon Frosting

Ingredients:

Earl Grey Cupcakes:

- 1 cup whole milk
- 4 Earl Grey tea bags
- 1/2 cup unsalted butter, softened
- 1 cup granulated sugar
- 2 large eggs
- 1 teaspoon vanilla extract
- 1 3/4 cups all-purpose flour
- 1 1/2 teaspoons baking powder
- 1/4 teaspoon salt

Lemon Frosting:

- 1 cup unsalted butter, softened
- 4 cups powdered sugar
- 2 tablespoons fresh lemon juice
- 1 teaspoon lemon zest
- Yellow food coloring (optional)

Instructions:

Infuse Milk with Earl Grey Tea:
- Heat the milk until it's warm but not boiling. Steep the Earl Grey tea bags in the warm milk for about 15-20 minutes. Remove the tea bags and allow the milk to cool.

Preheat Oven:
- Preheat your oven to 350°F (175°C). Line a muffin tin with cupcake liners.

Mix Dry Ingredients for Cupcakes:
- In a medium bowl, whisk together the flour, baking powder, and salt.

Cream Butter and Sugar for Cupcakes:
- In a large bowl, cream together the softened butter and granulated sugar until light and fluffy.

Add Eggs, Vanilla, and Earl Grey Milk:
- Add the eggs one at a time, beating well after each addition. Stir in the vanilla extract. Alternately add the dry ingredients and the Earl Grey-infused milk, starting and ending with the dry ingredients. Mix until just combined.

Fill Cupcake Liners:
- Divide the batter evenly among the cupcake liners, filling each about two-thirds full.

Bake Cupcakes:
- Bake in the preheated oven for 18-20 minutes or until a toothpick inserted into the center comes out clean.

Cool Cupcakes:
- Allow the Earl Grey cupcakes to cool in the muffin tin for 5 minutes, then transfer them to a wire rack to cool completely.

Make Lemon Frosting:
- In a large bowl, beat together the softened butter, powdered sugar, fresh lemon juice, and lemon zest until smooth and creamy. Add yellow food coloring if desired for a vibrant lemon color.

Frost Cupcakes:
- Once the cupcakes are completely cooled, frost them with the lemon frosting.

Garnish (Optional):
- Optionally, garnish with additional lemon zest or a small wedge of lemon for decoration.

Serve and Enjoy:
- Once frosted and garnished, serve and savor these delightful Earl Grey cupcakes with lemon frosting!

Tips:

- Adjust the steeping time for the Earl Grey tea according to your preference for tea strength.
- Use fresh lemon juice for a zesty and vibrant lemon flavor in the frosting.
- To enhance the citrus flavor, consider adding a bit more lemon zest to the frosting.

These Earl Grey cupcakes with lemon frosting offer a delightful blend of tea-infused sweetness and citrusy tang. They are perfect for tea lovers and those who appreciate a unique flavor combination. Enjoy the elegant and aromatic taste of Earl Grey in a cupcake!

Seasonal Specials:
Spiced Apple Cider Cupcakes

Ingredients:

Spiced Apple Cider Cupcakes:

- 1 1/2 cups all-purpose flour
- 1 1/2 teaspoons baking powder
- 1/2 teaspoon baking soda
- 1/4 teaspoon salt
- 1 teaspoon ground cinnamon
- 1/2 teaspoon ground nutmeg
- 1/4 teaspoon ground cloves
- 1/2 cup unsalted butter, softened
- 1 cup granulated sugar
- 2 large eggs
- 1 teaspoon vanilla extract
- 1 cup apple cider, reduced to 1/2 cup and cooled
- 1/2 cup buttermilk

Cinnamon Cream Cheese Frosting:

- 8 oz cream cheese, softened
- 1/2 cup unsalted butter, softened
- 4 cups powdered sugar
- 1 teaspoon ground cinnamon
- 1 teaspoon vanilla extract

Instructions:

Reduce Apple Cider:
- In a saucepan, bring 1 cup of apple cider to a boil. Reduce the heat and simmer until it's reduced to 1/2 cup. Allow it to cool before using.

Preheat Oven:
- Preheat your oven to 350°F (175°C). Line a muffin tin with cupcake liners.

Mix Dry Ingredients for Cupcakes:
- In a medium bowl, whisk together the flour, baking powder, baking soda, salt, cinnamon, nutmeg, and cloves.

Cream Butter and Sugar for Cupcakes:
- In a large bowl, cream together the softened butter and granulated sugar until light and fluffy.

Add Eggs and Vanilla for Cupcakes:
- Add the eggs one at a time, beating well after each addition. Stir in the vanilla extract.

Combine Reduced Apple Cider and Buttermilk:
- In a separate bowl, combine the reduced apple cider and buttermilk.

Add Dry Ingredients and Cider Mixture:
- Gradually add the dry ingredients to the wet ingredients, alternating with the cider and buttermilk mixture. Begin and end with the dry ingredients, mixing until just combined. Do not overmix.

Fill Cupcake Liners:
- Divide the batter evenly among the cupcake liners, filling each about two-thirds full.

Bake Cupcakes:
- Bake in the preheated oven for 18-20 minutes or until a toothpick inserted into the center comes out clean.

Cool Cupcakes:
- Allow the spiced apple cider cupcakes to cool in the muffin tin for 5 minutes, then transfer them to a wire rack to cool completely.

Make Cinnamon Cream Cheese Frosting:
- In a large bowl, beat together the softened cream cheese, softened butter, powdered sugar, ground cinnamon, and vanilla extract until smooth and creamy.

Frost Cupcakes:
- Once the cupcakes are completely cooled, frost them with the cinnamon cream cheese frosting.

Garnish (Optional):
- Optionally, garnish with a sprinkle of ground cinnamon on top for added flavor and decoration.

Serve and Enjoy:
- Once frosted and garnished, serve and relish these spiced apple cider cupcakes with cinnamon cream cheese frosting!

Tips:

- Experiment with different varieties of apples or use homemade apple cider for a personalized touch.

- Adjust the amount of ground spices in the cupcakes according to your taste preferences.
- For a stronger apple flavor, add a few tablespoons of applesauce to the cupcake batter.

These spiced apple cider cupcakes bring the warmth of fall flavors to your dessert table. Enjoy the combination of aromatic spices and apple cider in every moist and delicious bite!

Pumpkin Cheesecake Cupcakes

Ingredients:

Pumpkin Cheesecake Cupcakes:

- 1 1/2 cups graham cracker crumbs
- 1/4 cup unsalted butter, melted
- 16 oz cream cheese, softened
- 3/4 cup granulated sugar
- 1 cup canned pumpkin puree
- 1 teaspoon vanilla extract
- 1/2 teaspoon ground cinnamon
- 1/4 teaspoon ground nutmeg
- 1/4 teaspoon ground cloves
- 1/4 teaspoon salt
- 3 large eggs

Whipped Cream Topping:

- 1 cup heavy cream
- 2 tablespoons powdered sugar
- 1/2 teaspoon vanilla extract

Instructions:

Preheat Oven:
- Preheat your oven to 325°F (160°C). Line a muffin tin with cupcake liners.

Make Graham Cracker Crust:
- In a bowl, combine graham cracker crumbs and melted butter. Press the mixture into the bottom of each cupcake liner, creating the crust.

Prepare Cream Cheese Filling:
- In a large bowl, beat the cream cheese until smooth. Add sugar and mix until well combined.

Add Pumpkin and Spices:
- Add the canned pumpkin, vanilla extract, ground cinnamon, nutmeg, cloves, and salt to the cream cheese mixture. Mix until smooth.

Add Eggs:

- Add the eggs one at a time, beating well after each addition. Ensure the batter is thoroughly combined but avoid overmixing.

Fill Cupcake Liners:
- Divide the pumpkin cheesecake batter evenly among the cupcake liners, on top of the graham cracker crust.

Bake Cupcakes:
- Bake in the preheated oven for about 20-25 minutes or until the center is set. A slight jiggle is normal.

Cool and Refrigerate:
- Allow the cupcakes to cool in the muffin tin for 10 minutes, then transfer them to a wire rack. Refrigerate for at least 2 hours or until fully chilled.

Prepare Whipped Cream Topping:
- In a chilled bowl, whip the heavy cream, powdered sugar, and vanilla extract until stiff peaks form.

Frost Cupcakes:
- Once the pumpkin cheesecake cupcakes are fully chilled, pipe or spoon the whipped cream on top of each cupcake.

Serve and Enjoy:
- Serve these delightful pumpkin cheesecake cupcakes and enjoy the rich, creamy flavor!

Tips:

- For a stronger spice flavor, adjust the quantities of cinnamon, nutmeg, and cloves according to your preference.
- Chill the cupcakes for a longer period if you prefer a firmer texture.
- Garnish with a sprinkle of cinnamon or a drizzle of caramel sauce for added flair.

These pumpkin cheesecake cupcakes are a delicious and individual-sized treat perfect for fall or any time you're craving the delightful combination of pumpkin and creamy cheesecake. Enjoy the rich and spiced flavors with every bite!

Gingerbread Cupcakes

Ingredients:

Gingerbread Cupcakes:

- 1 1/2 cups all-purpose flour
- 1 teaspoon ground ginger
- 1 teaspoon ground cinnamon
- 1/4 teaspoon ground cloves
- 1/4 teaspoon ground nutmeg
- 1/4 teaspoon salt
- 1/2 cup unsalted butter, softened
- 1/2 cup brown sugar, packed
- 1/2 cup molasses
- 2 large eggs
- 1 teaspoon vanilla extract
- 1/2 cup buttermilk

Cream Cheese Frosting:

- 8 oz cream cheese, softened
- 1/2 cup unsalted butter, softened
- 4 cups powdered sugar
- 1 teaspoon vanilla extract

Instructions:

Preheat Oven:
- Preheat your oven to 350°F (175°C). Line a muffin tin with cupcake liners.

Mix Dry Ingredients for Cupcakes:
- In a medium bowl, whisk together the flour, ground ginger, ground cinnamon, ground cloves, ground nutmeg, and salt.

Cream Butter and Sugar for Cupcakes:
- In a large bowl, cream together the softened butter and brown sugar until light and fluffy.

Add Molasses, Eggs, and Vanilla for Cupcakes:
- Add the molasses, eggs, and vanilla extract to the creamed butter and sugar. Mix until well combined.

Combine Dry Ingredients Alternately with Buttermilk:
- Gradually add the dry ingredients to the wet ingredients, alternating with the buttermilk. Begin and end with the dry ingredients, mixing until just combined. Do not overmix.

Fill Cupcake Liners:
- Divide the batter evenly among the cupcake liners, filling each about two-thirds full.

Bake Cupcakes:
- Bake in the preheated oven for 18-20 minutes or until a toothpick inserted into the center comes out clean.

Cool Cupcakes:
- Allow the gingerbread cupcakes to cool in the muffin tin for 5 minutes, then transfer them to a wire rack to cool completely.

Make Cream Cheese Frosting:
- In a large bowl, beat together the softened cream cheese, softened butter, powdered sugar, and vanilla extract until smooth and creamy.

Frost Cupcakes:
- Once the cupcakes are completely cooled, frost them with the cream cheese frosting.

Garnish (Optional):
- Optionally, garnish with a sprinkle of ground cinnamon or gingerbread cookie crumbs on top.

Serve and Enjoy:
- Once frosted and garnished, serve and relish these festive gingerbread cupcakes!

Tips:

- Adjust the spice levels by increasing or decreasing the amount of ginger, cinnamon, cloves, or nutmeg.
- For a more pronounced molasses flavor, use dark molasses.
- Decorate with gingerbread cookies or holiday-themed sprinkles for a festive touch.

These gingerbread cupcakes capture the warm and spicy flavors of the holiday season. Enjoy the delightful combination of ginger, cinnamon, and molasses in a moist and tender cupcake, topped with creamy cream cheese frosting. Perfect for festive occasions or whenever you're in the mood for a cozy treat!

Cranberry White Chocolate Cupcakes

Ingredients:

Cranberry White Chocolate Cupcakes:

- 1 1/2 cups all-purpose flour
- 1 1/2 teaspoons baking powder
- 1/4 teaspoon salt
- 1/2 cup unsalted butter, softened
- 1 cup granulated sugar
- 2 large eggs
- 1 teaspoon vanilla extract
- 1/2 cup whole milk
- 1/2 cup dried cranberries, chopped
- 1/2 cup white chocolate chips

White Chocolate Cream Cheese Frosting:

- 8 oz cream cheese, softened
- 1/2 cup unsalted butter, softened
- 2 cups powdered sugar
- 1 teaspoon vanilla extract
- 1/2 cup white chocolate chips, melted and cooled

Instructions:

Preheat Oven:
- Preheat your oven to 350°F (175°C). Line a muffin tin with cupcake liners.

Mix Dry Ingredients for Cupcakes:
- In a medium bowl, whisk together the flour, baking powder, and salt.

Cream Butter and Sugar for Cupcakes:
- In a large bowl, cream together the softened butter and granulated sugar until light and fluffy.

Add Eggs and Vanilla for Cupcakes:
- Add the eggs one at a time, beating well after each addition. Stir in the vanilla extract.

Combine Dry Ingredients Alternately with Milk:

- Gradually add the dry ingredients to the wet ingredients, alternating with the whole milk. Begin and end with the dry ingredients, mixing until just combined. Do not overmix.

Fold in Cranberries and White Chocolate Chips:
- Gently fold in the chopped dried cranberries and white chocolate chips until evenly distributed throughout the batter.

Fill Cupcake Liners:
- Divide the batter evenly among the cupcake liners, filling each about two-thirds full.

Bake Cupcakes:
- Bake in the preheated oven for 18-20 minutes or until a toothpick inserted into the center comes out clean.

Cool Cupcakes:
- Allow the cranberry white chocolate cupcakes to cool in the muffin tin for 5 minutes, then transfer them to a wire rack to cool completely.

Make White Chocolate Cream Cheese Frosting:
- In a large bowl, beat together the softened cream cheese, softened butter, powdered sugar, and vanilla extract until smooth and creamy. Add the melted and cooled white chocolate, mixing until well combined.

Frost Cupcakes:
- Once the cupcakes are completely cooled, frost them with the white chocolate cream cheese frosting.

Garnish (Optional):
- Optionally, garnish with additional dried cranberries or white chocolate shavings on top for a decorative touch.

Serve and Enjoy:
- Once frosted and garnished, serve and enjoy these delectable cranberry white chocolate cupcakes!

Tips:

- Ensure the dried cranberries are chopped into smaller pieces for even distribution in the batter.
- Melt the white chocolate chips gently, either in a double boiler or in short intervals in the microwave, stirring to avoid burning.
- Adjust the sweetness of the frosting by adding more or less powdered sugar according to your taste.

These cranberry white chocolate cupcakes offer a delightful blend of tartness from the cranberries and sweetness from the white chocolate. They are perfect for holiday gatherings or any occasion where you want to indulge in a festive treat. Enjoy the harmonious pairing of cranberries and white chocolate in every bite!

Peppermint Mocha Cupcakes

Ingredients:

Peppermint Mocha Cupcakes:

- 1 1/2 cups all-purpose flour
- 1/2 cup unsweetened cocoa powder
- 1 teaspoon baking powder
- 1/2 teaspoon baking soda
- 1/4 teaspoon salt
- 1/2 cup unsalted butter, softened
- 1 cup granulated sugar
- 2 large eggs
- 1 teaspoon vanilla extract
- 1/2 cup buttermilk
- 1/2 cup strong brewed coffee, cooled
- 1/4 cup peppermint extract
- 1/2 cup mini chocolate chips

Peppermint Mocha Buttercream Frosting:

- 1 cup unsalted butter, softened
- 3 cups powdered sugar
- 1/4 cup unsweetened cocoa powder
- 1/4 cup strong brewed coffee, cooled
- 1/2 teaspoon peppermint extract
- Crushed candy canes for garnish

Instructions:

Preheat Oven:
- Preheat your oven to 350°F (175°C). Line a muffin tin with cupcake liners.

Mix Dry Ingredients for Cupcakes:
- In a medium bowl, whisk together the flour, cocoa powder, baking powder, baking soda, and salt.

Cream Butter and Sugar for Cupcakes:

- In a large bowl, cream together the softened butter and granulated sugar until light and fluffy.

Add Eggs and Vanilla for Cupcakes:
- Add the eggs one at a time, beating well after each addition. Stir in the vanilla extract.

Combine Dry Ingredients Alternately with Buttermilk and Coffee:
- Gradually add the dry ingredients to the wet ingredients, alternating with the buttermilk and coffee. Begin and end with the dry ingredients, mixing until just combined. Do not overmix.

Add Peppermint Extract and Chocolate Chips:
- Stir in the peppermint extract and fold in the mini chocolate chips until evenly distributed throughout the batter.

Fill Cupcake Liners:
- Divide the batter evenly among the cupcake liners, filling each about two-thirds full.

Bake Cupcakes:
- Bake in the preheated oven for 18-20 minutes or until a toothpick inserted into the center comes out clean.

Cool Cupcakes:
- Allow the peppermint mocha cupcakes to cool in the muffin tin for 5 minutes, then transfer them to a wire rack to cool completely.

Make Peppermint Mocha Buttercream Frosting:
- In a large bowl, beat together the softened butter, powdered sugar, cocoa powder, brewed coffee, and peppermint extract until smooth and creamy.

Frost Cupcakes:
- Once the cupcakes are completely cooled, frost them with the peppermint mocha buttercream frosting.

Garnish with Crushed Candy Canes:
- Sprinkle crushed candy canes on top of the frosting for a festive and minty garnish.

Serve and Enjoy:
- Once frosted and garnished, serve and indulge in these delightful peppermint mocha cupcakes!

Tips:

- Adjust the amount of peppermint extract according to your taste preference.
- Ensure the brewed coffee is cooled before adding it to the batter and frosting.

- For a more pronounced mocha flavor, you can increase the amount of cocoa powder in the frosting.

These peppermint mocha cupcakes are a perfect combination of rich chocolate, refreshing peppermint, and a hint of coffee. They make a festive and flavorful treat for the holiday season or any time you crave a delightful blend of chocolate and mint. Enjoy the delightful taste of a peppermint mocha in cupcake form!

Eggnog Cupcakes

Ingredients:

Eggnog Cupcakes:

- 1 1/2 cups all-purpose flour
- 1 1/2 teaspoons baking powder
- 1/4 teaspoon salt
- 1/2 cup unsalted butter, softened
- 1 cup granulated sugar
- 2 large eggs
- 1 teaspoon vanilla extract
- 1/2 cup eggnog
- 1/4 cup spiced rum (optional)
- 1/4 teaspoon ground nutmeg
- 1/4 teaspoon ground cinnamon

Eggnog Cream Cheese Frosting:

- 8 oz cream cheese, softened
- 1/2 cup unsalted butter, softened
- 4 cups powdered sugar
- 1/4 cup eggnog
- 1/4 teaspoon ground nutmeg
- 1/4 teaspoon ground cinnamon

Instructions:

Preheat Oven:
- Preheat your oven to 350°F (175°C). Line a muffin tin with cupcake liners.

Mix Dry Ingredients for Cupcakes:
- In a medium bowl, whisk together the flour, baking powder, and salt.

Cream Butter and Sugar for Cupcakes:
- In a large bowl, cream together the softened butter and granulated sugar until light and fluffy.

Add Eggs and Vanilla for Cupcakes:

- Add the eggs one at a time, beating well after each addition. Stir in the vanilla extract.

Combine Dry Ingredients Alternately with Eggnog and Rum:
- Gradually add the dry ingredients to the wet ingredients, alternating with the eggnog and spiced rum (if using). Begin and end with the dry ingredients, mixing until just combined. Do not overmix.

Add Nutmeg and Cinnamon:
- Stir in the ground nutmeg and ground cinnamon until evenly distributed throughout the batter.

Fill Cupcake Liners:
- Divide the batter evenly among the cupcake liners, filling each about two-thirds full.

Bake Cupcakes:
- Bake in the preheated oven for 18-20 minutes or until a toothpick inserted into the center comes out clean.

Cool Cupcakes:
- Allow the eggnog cupcakes to cool in the muffin tin for 5 minutes, then transfer them to a wire rack to cool completely.

Make Eggnog Cream Cheese Frosting:
- In a large bowl, beat together the softened cream cheese, softened butter, powdered sugar, eggnog, ground nutmeg, and ground cinnamon until smooth and creamy.

Frost Cupcakes:
- Once the cupcakes are completely cooled, frost them with the eggnog cream cheese frosting.

Garnish (Optional):
- Optionally, garnish with a sprinkle of ground nutmeg on top for a festive touch.

Serve and Enjoy:
- Once frosted and garnished, serve and savor these delicious eggnog cupcakes!

Tips:

- Adjust the amount of spiced rum according to your preference for an extra kick.
- Ensure the eggnog and spiced rum are at room temperature before adding them to the batter.

- For a smoother frosting, make sure the cream cheese and butter are well softened.

These eggnog cupcakes capture the rich and creamy flavors of the holiday season. With a hint of nutmeg, cinnamon, and optional spiced rum, they make a delightful treat for festive occasions or whenever you want to indulge in the taste of eggnog. Enjoy the warmth and flavor of the holidays in every bite!

Nutty Goodness:
Pecan Pie Cupcakes

Ingredients:

Pecan Pie Cupcakes:

- 1 cup all-purpose flour
- 1/2 cup unsalted butter, melted
- 1 cup packed brown sugar
- 2 large eggs
- 1 teaspoon vanilla extract
- 1 cup chopped pecans

Pecan Pie Filling:

- 1/2 cup packed brown sugar
- 1/4 cup corn syrup
- 2 tablespoons unsalted butter, melted
- 1 teaspoon vanilla extract
- 1 cup chopped pecans

Whipped Cream Topping:

- 1 cup heavy cream
- 2 tablespoons powdered sugar
- 1/2 teaspoon vanilla extract

Instructions:

Preheat Oven and Prepare Cupcake Liners:
- Preheat your oven to 350°F (175°C). Line a muffin tin with cupcake liners.

Make Pecan Pie Cupcake Base:
- In a bowl, combine melted butter, brown sugar, eggs, and vanilla extract. Stir in the flour until just combined. Fold in the chopped pecans.

Fill Cupcake Liners:
- Divide the batter evenly among the cupcake liners, filling each about two-thirds full.

Make Pecan Pie Filling:

- In a separate bowl, mix together brown sugar, corn syrup, melted butter, vanilla extract, and chopped pecans.

Add Pecan Pie Filling on Top:
- Spoon a small amount of the pecan pie filling on top of each cupcake, covering the batter.

Bake Cupcakes:
- Bake in the preheated oven for 20-25 minutes or until a toothpick inserted into the center comes out clean. The pecan pie filling will set as the cupcakes bake.

Cool Cupcakes:
- Allow the pecan pie cupcakes to cool in the muffin tin for 10 minutes, then transfer them to a wire rack to cool completely.

Make Whipped Cream Topping:
- In a chilled bowl, whip the heavy cream, powdered sugar, and vanilla extract until stiff peaks form.

Top with Whipped Cream:
- Once the cupcakes are completely cooled, pipe or spoon the whipped cream on top of each cupcake.

Garnish (Optional):
- Optionally, garnish with additional chopped pecans or a drizzle of caramel sauce on top.

Serve and Enjoy:
- Once topped and garnished, serve and relish these delicious pecan pie cupcakes!

Tips:

- Toast the chopped pecans before adding them to the batter for enhanced flavor.
- For an extra touch of indulgence, serve the cupcakes warm with a scoop of vanilla ice cream.
- Adjust the sweetness of the whipped cream according to your taste preference by adding more or less powdered sugar.

These pecan pie cupcakes are a delightful twist on the classic pecan pie, combining the flavors of a buttery pecan pie filling with a moist cupcake base. They are perfect for dessert lovers who enjoy the rich, nutty taste of pecans. Enjoy the essence of pecan pie in a convenient cupcake form!

Almond Joy Cupcakes

Ingredients:

Chocolate Cupcakes:

- 1 1/2 cups all-purpose flour
- 1 cup granulated sugar
- 1/2 cup unsweetened cocoa powder
- 1 teaspoon baking powder
- 1/2 teaspoon baking soda
- 1/4 teaspoon salt
- 1 cup buttermilk
- 1/2 cup vegetable oil
- 2 large eggs
- 2 teaspoons vanilla extract

Coconut Almond Filling:

- 1 cup sweetened shredded coconut
- 1/2 cup sweetened condensed milk
- 1/4 cup chopped almonds
- 1 teaspoon vanilla extract

Chocolate Ganache:

- 1/2 cup heavy cream
- 1 cup semi-sweet chocolate chips

Almond Joy Topping:

- Almond halves
- Sweetened shredded coconut

Instructions:

Preheat Oven and Prepare Cupcake Liners:

- Preheat your oven to 350°F (175°C). Line a muffin tin with cupcake liners.

Make Chocolate Cupcake Batter:
- In a large bowl, whisk together flour, sugar, cocoa powder, baking powder, baking soda, and salt. In a separate bowl, whisk together buttermilk, vegetable oil, eggs, and vanilla extract. Pour the wet ingredients into the dry ingredients and mix until just combined.

Fill Cupcake Liners:
- Divide the batter evenly among the cupcake liners, filling each about two-thirds full.

Bake Cupcakes:
- Bake in the preheated oven for 18-20 minutes or until a toothpick inserted into the center comes out clean. Allow cupcakes to cool completely.

Make Coconut Almond Filling:
- In a bowl, combine shredded coconut, sweetened condensed milk, chopped almonds, and vanilla extract. Mix until well combined.

Create a Well in Cupcakes:
- Once the cupcakes are cooled, use a knife or cupcake corer to create a well in the center of each cupcake.

Fill with Coconut Almond Mixture:
- Spoon or pipe the coconut almond filling into the well of each cupcake.

Make Chocolate Ganache:
- In a saucepan, heat the heavy cream until it just begins to simmer. Pour the hot cream over the chocolate chips in a heatproof bowl. Let it sit for a minute, then stir until smooth and glossy.

Dip Cupcakes in Chocolate Ganache:
- Dip the tops of each cupcake into the chocolate ganache, allowing any excess to drip off.

Top with Almonds and Coconut:
- Immediately after dipping, place an almond half on top of each cupcake, and sprinkle with sweetened shredded coconut.

Chill Cupcakes:
- Place the cupcakes in the refrigerator for the ganache to set.

Serve and Enjoy:
- Once set, serve and enjoy these indulgent Almond Joy cupcakes!

Tips:

- For a more intense coconut flavor, you can add coconut extract to the chocolate cupcake batter.
- Toast the shredded coconut and chopped almonds before adding them to the filling for enhanced flavor.
- Experiment with dark chocolate or milk chocolate ganache based on your preference.

These Almond Joy cupcakes capture the essence of the classic candy bar with the combination of chocolate, coconut, and almonds. Perfect for those who love the iconic flavors of Almond Joy in a delightful cupcake form. Enjoy the sweet and nutty goodness in every bite!

Hazelnut Chocolate Cupcakes

Ingredients:

Chocolate Hazelnut Cupcakes:

- 1 1/2 cups all-purpose flour
- 1/2 cup unsweetened cocoa powder
- 1 1/2 teaspoons baking powder
- 1/2 teaspoon baking soda
- 1/4 teaspoon salt
- 1/2 cup unsalted butter, softened
- 1 cup granulated sugar
- 2 large eggs
- 1 teaspoon vanilla extract
- 1 cup buttermilk
- 1/2 cup chopped hazelnuts

Chocolate Hazelnut Ganache:

- 1/2 cup heavy cream
- 1 cup semi-sweet chocolate chips
- 1/4 cup chopped hazelnuts (for garnish)

Hazelnut Cream Cheese Frosting:

- 8 oz cream cheese, softened
- 1/2 cup unsalted butter, softened
- 4 cups powdered sugar
- 1/2 cup hazelnut spread (e.g., Nutella)
- 1 teaspoon vanilla extract

Instructions:

Preheat Oven and Prepare Cupcake Liners:
- Preheat your oven to 350°F (175°C). Line a muffin tin with cupcake liners.

Make Chocolate Hazelnut Cupcake Batter:

- In a large bowl, whisk together flour, cocoa powder, baking powder, baking soda, and salt. In another bowl, cream together softened butter and granulated sugar until light and fluffy. Add eggs one at a time, beating well after each addition. Stir in vanilla extract. Gradually add the dry ingredients to the wet ingredients, alternating with buttermilk. Mix until just combined, then fold in the chopped hazelnuts.

Fill Cupcake Liners:
- Divide the batter evenly among the cupcake liners, filling each about two-thirds full.

Bake Cupcakes:
- Bake in the preheated oven for 18-20 minutes or until a toothpick inserted into the center comes out clean. Allow cupcakes to cool completely.

Make Chocolate Hazelnut Ganache:
- In a saucepan, heat the heavy cream until it just begins to simmer. Pour the hot cream over the chocolate chips in a heatproof bowl. Let it sit for a minute, then stir until smooth and glossy.

Dip Cupcakes in Chocolate Ganache:
- Dip the tops of each cupcake into the chocolate hazelnut ganache, allowing any excess to drip off.

Make Hazelnut Cream Cheese Frosting:
- In a large bowl, beat together the softened cream cheese, softened butter, powdered sugar, hazelnut spread, and vanilla extract until smooth and creamy

Frost Cupcakes:
- Once the cupcakes are completely cooled and the ganache is set, pipe or spread the hazelnut cream cheese frosting on top.

Garnish with Chopped Hazelnuts:
- Sprinkle chopped hazelnuts on top of each cupcake for a delightful garnish.

Serve and Enjoy:
- Once frosted and garnished, serve and indulge in these scrumptious hazelnut chocolate cupcakes!

Tips:

- Toast the chopped hazelnuts before adding them to the cupcake batter for a richer flavor.

- Adjust the amount of hazelnut spread in the frosting according to your taste preference.
- Drizzle extra chocolate ganache on top or garnish with whole hazelnuts for an elegant touch.

These hazelnut chocolate cupcakes bring together the delightful combination of rich chocolate and nutty hazelnuts. With a luscious hazelnut cream cheese frosting and a glossy chocolate ganache, they make a decadent treat for any occasion. Enjoy the indulgent flavors of hazelnut and chocolate in each delectable bite!

Pistachio Rose Cupcakes

Ingredients:

Pistachio Rose Cupcakes:

- 1 1/2 cups all-purpose flour
- 1/2 cup pistachio flour (ground pistachios)
- 1 1/2 teaspoons baking powder
- 1/2 teaspoon baking soda
- 1/4 teaspoon salt
- 1/2 cup unsalted butter, softened
- 1 cup granulated sugar
- 2 large eggs
- 1 teaspoon vanilla extract
- 1 cup buttermilk
- 1/4 cup rosewater
- 1/2 cup chopped pistachios (for garnish)

Rosewater Buttercream Frosting:

- 1 cup unsalted butter, softened
- 4 cups powdered sugar
- 1/4 cup rosewater
- A few drops of pink food coloring (optional)
- Chopped pistachios and edible rose petals for decoration

Instructions:

Preheat Oven and Prepare Cupcake Liners:
- Preheat your oven to 350°F (175°C). Line a muffin tin with cupcake liners.

Make Pistachio Rose Cupcake Batter:
- In a bowl, whisk together the flour, pistachio flour, baking powder, baking soda, and salt. In another large bowl, cream together the softened butter and granulated sugar until light and fluffy. Add the eggs one at a time, beating well after each addition. Stir in the vanilla extract. Gradually add the dry ingredients to the wet ingredients, alternating with buttermilk. Mix

until just combined. Stir in the rosewater until evenly distributed. Fold in the chopped pistachios.

Fill Cupcake Liners:
- Divide the batter evenly among the cupcake liners, filling each about two-thirds full.

Bake Cupcakes:
- Bake in the preheated oven for 18-20 minutes or until a toothpick inserted into the center comes out clean. Allow cupcakes to cool completely.

Make Rosewater Buttercream Frosting:
- In a large bowl, beat together the softened butter, powdered sugar, rosewater, and pink food coloring (if using) until smooth and creamy.

Frost Cupcakes:
- Once the cupcakes are completely cooled, pipe or spread the rosewater buttercream frosting on top.

Garnish with Pistachios and Edible Rose Petals:
- Sprinkle chopped pistachios on top of each cupcake and decorate with edible rose petals for a touch of elegance.

Serve and Enjoy:
- Once frosted and garnished, serve and savor these delightful pistachio rose cupcakes!

Tips:

- Ensure the pistachios are finely ground for a smooth texture in the cupcakes.
- Adjust the amount of rosewater in the frosting based on your preference for a subtle or more pronounced rose flavor.
- For an extra pop of color, add a drop or two of natural pink food coloring to the cupcake batter.

These pistachio rose cupcakes offer a unique and sophisticated flavor combination, with the nuttiness of pistachios and the floral notes of rosewater. Topped with a fragrant rosewater buttercream and garnished with pistachios and edible rose petals, they make a beautiful and delicious treat for special occasions or any day you want to indulge in a delightful cupcake. Enjoy the harmonious blend of pistachio and rose in each bite!

Maple Walnut Cupcakes

Ingredients:

Maple Walnut Cupcakes:

- 1 1/2 cups all-purpose flour
- 1 teaspoon baking powder
- 1/2 teaspoon baking soda
- 1/4 teaspoon salt
- 1/2 cup unsalted butter, softened
- 1 cup granulated sugar
- 2 large eggs
- 1 teaspoon vanilla extract
- 1/2 cup pure maple syrup
- 1/2 cup buttermilk
- 1 cup chopped walnuts

Maple Cream Cheese Frosting:

- 8 oz cream cheese, softened
- 1/2 cup unsalted butter, softened
- 4 cups powdered sugar
- 1/4 cup pure maple syrup
- 1 teaspoon vanilla extract
- Chopped walnuts for garnish

Instructions:

Preheat Oven and Prepare Cupcake Liners:
- Preheat your oven to 350°F (175°C). Line a muffin tin with cupcake liners.

Make Maple Walnut Cupcake Batter:
- In a bowl, whisk together the flour, baking powder, baking soda, and salt. In another large bowl, cream together the softened butter and granulated sugar until light and fluffy. Add the eggs one at a time, beating well after each addition. Stir in the vanilla extract. Mix in the pure maple syrup. Gradually add the dry ingredients to the wet ingredients, alternating with buttermilk. Mix until just combined. Fold in the chopped walnuts.

Fill Cupcake Liners:

- Divide the batter evenly among the cupcake liners, filling each about two-thirds full.

Bake Cupcakes:
- Bake in the preheated oven for 18-20 minutes or until a toothpick inserted into the center comes out clean. Allow cupcakes to cool completely.

Make Maple Cream Cheese Frosting:
- In a large bowl, beat together the softened cream cheese, softened butter, powdered sugar, pure maple syrup, and vanilla extract until smooth and creamy.

Frost Cupcakes:
- Once the cupcakes are completely cooled, pipe or spread the maple cream cheese frosting on top.

Garnish with Chopped Walnuts:
- Sprinkle chopped walnuts on top of each cupcake for a delightful garnish.

Serve and Enjoy:
- Once frosted and garnished, serve and savor these delicious maple walnut cupcakes!

Tips:

- Use pure maple syrup for an authentic maple flavor in both the cupcakes and the frosting.
- Toast the chopped walnuts before adding them to the cupcake batter for enhanced flavor.
- Adjust the sweetness of the frosting by adding more or less powdered sugar to suit your taste.

These maple walnut cupcakes offer a delightful blend of rich maple flavor and the nutty crunch of walnuts. Topped with a luscious maple cream cheese frosting and garnished with chopped walnuts, they make a perfect treat for maple and nut lovers alike. Enjoy the warm and comforting taste of maple in every bite!

Peanut Butter Banana Cupcakes

Ingredients:

Peanut Butter Banana Cupcakes:

- 1 1/2 cups all-purpose flour
- 1 teaspoon baking powder
- 1/2 teaspoon baking soda
- 1/4 teaspoon salt
- 1/2 cup unsalted butter, softened
- 1 cup granulated sugar
- 2 large eggs
- 1 teaspoon vanilla extract
- 3 ripe bananas, mashed
- 1/2 cup creamy peanut butter
- 1/2 cup buttermilk

Peanut Butter Cream Cheese Frosting:

- 8 oz cream cheese, softened
- 1/2 cup unsalted butter, softened
- 1 cup creamy peanut butter
- 4 cups powdered sugar
- 1 teaspoon vanilla extract
- Crushed peanuts for garnish (optional)

Instructions:

Preheat Oven and Prepare Cupcake Liners:
- Preheat your oven to 350°F (175°C). Line a muffin tin with cupcake liners.

Make Peanut Butter Banana Cupcake Batter:
- In a bowl, whisk together the flour, baking powder, baking soda, and salt. In another large bowl, cream together the softened butter and granulated sugar until light and fluffy. Add the eggs one at a time, beating well after each addition. Stir in the vanilla extract. Mix in the mashed bananas, peanut butter, and buttermilk. Gradually add the dry ingredients to the wet ingredients, mixing until just combined.

Fill Cupcake Liners:

- Divide the batter evenly among the cupcake liners, filling each about two-thirds full.

Bake Cupcakes:
- Bake in the preheated oven for 18-20 minutes or until a toothpick inserted into the center comes out clean. Allow cupcakes to cool completely.

Make Peanut Butter Cream Cheese Frosting:
- In a large bowl, beat together the softened cream cheese, softened butter, creamy peanut butter, powdered sugar, and vanilla extract until smooth and creamy.

Frost Cupcakes:
- Once the cupcakes are completely cooled, pipe or spread the peanut butter cream cheese frosting on top.

Garnish with Crushed Peanuts (Optional):
- Optionally, garnish with crushed peanuts on top of each cupcake for added texture.

Serve and Enjoy:
- Once frosted and garnished, serve and relish these delicious peanut butter banana cupcakes!

Tips:

- Use ripe bananas for a more intense banana flavor in the cupcakes.
- Adjust the amount of peanut butter in the frosting based on your preference for a stronger or milder peanut butter taste.
- For a fun twist, add a dollop of banana slices on top of the frosting before serving.

These peanut butter banana cupcakes offer a delightful combination of nutty peanut butter and sweet banana. Topped with a creamy peanut butter cream cheese frosting and optionally garnished with crushed peanuts, they make a perfect treat for those who love the classic pairing of peanut butter and banana. Enjoy the rich and comforting flavors in every bite!

Cupcake and Muffin Combinations:

Blueberry Cheesecake Muffins

Ingredients:

Blueberry Muffin Batter:

- 1 1/2 cups all-purpose flour
- 1/2 cup granulated sugar
- 2 teaspoons baking powder
- 1/2 teaspoon baking soda
- 1/4 teaspoon salt
- 1 cup buttermilk
- 1/4 cup unsalted butter, melted
- 1 large egg
- 1 teaspoon vanilla extract
- 1 1/2 cups fresh or frozen blueberries

Cheesecake Filling:

- 8 oz cream cheese, softened
- 1/3 cup granulated sugar
- 1 large egg
- 1 teaspoon vanilla extract

Streusel Topping:

- 1/4 cup all-purpose flour
- 2 tablespoons unsalted butter, cold and cubed
- 2 tablespoons granulated sugar
- 1/4 teaspoon ground cinnamon

Instructions:

Preheat Oven and Prepare Muffin Tin:
- Preheat your oven to 375°F (190°C). Line a muffin tin with paper liners.

Make Cheesecake Filling:

- In a medium bowl, beat together the softened cream cheese, sugar, egg, and vanilla extract until smooth. Set aside.

Prepare Streusel Topping:
- In a small bowl, combine flour, cold cubed butter, sugar, and ground cinnamon. Use your fingers or a fork to mix until crumbly. Set aside.

Make Blueberry Muffin Batter:
- In a large bowl, whisk together flour, sugar, baking powder, baking soda, and salt. In another bowl, whisk together buttermilk, melted butter, egg, and vanilla extract. Pour the wet ingredients into the dry ingredients and mix until just combined. Gently fold in the blueberries.

Fill Muffin Cups:
- Spoon a small amount of the blueberry muffin batter into each muffin cup, filling each about one-third full.

Add Cheesecake Filling:
- Add a dollop of the cheesecake filling on top of the blueberry batter in each muffin cup.

Top with More Batter:
- Cover the cheesecake filling with more blueberry muffin batter, filling each cup almost to the top.

Sprinkle Streusel Topping:
- Sprinkle the streusel topping over the muffins, covering the batter.

Bake Muffins:
- Bake in the preheated oven for 20-25 minutes or until a toothpick inserted into the center comes out clean. Allow muffins to cool in the tin for 5 minutes, then transfer them to a wire rack to cool completely.

Serve and Enjoy:
- Once cooled, serve and enjoy these delightful blueberry cheesecake muffins!

Tips:

- If using frozen blueberries, do not thaw them before adding to the batter to prevent excess moisture.
- Adjust the amount of streusel topping based on your preference for a more or less crumbly texture.
- For added freshness, fold in a tablespoon of lemon zest into the blueberry muffin batter.

These blueberry cheesecake muffins combine the sweetness of blueberries with the rich creaminess of cheesecake, all topped with a cinnamon streusel for a delightful treat. Enjoy the burst of blueberry flavor and the creamy cheesecake surprise in each bite!

Chocolate Chip Cookie Dough Cupcakes

Ingredients:

Chocolate Chip Cupcakes:

- 1 1/2 cups all-purpose flour
- 1 teaspoon baking powder
- 1/2 teaspoon baking soda
- 1/4 teaspoon salt
- 1/2 cup unsalted butter, softened
- 1 cup granulated sugar
- 2 large eggs
- 2 teaspoons vanilla extract
- 1/2 cup sour cream
- 1/2 cup milk
- 1 cup mini chocolate chips

Cookie Dough Filling:

- 1/2 cup unsalted butter, softened
- 1/2 cup packed light brown sugar
- 1 cup all-purpose flour
- 1/4 teaspoon salt
- 1 cup mini chocolate chips

Cookie Dough Frosting:

- 1 cup unsalted butter, softened
- 1 cup packed light brown sugar
- 2 cups powdered sugar
- 1/2 cup all-purpose flour
- 1/4 teaspoon salt
- 1/4 cup milk
- 1 teaspoon vanilla extract
- 1 cup mini chocolate chips

Instructions:

Preheat Oven and Prepare Cupcake Liners:
- Preheat your oven to 350°F (175°C). Line a muffin tin with cupcake liners.

Make Chocolate Chip Cupcake Batter:
- In a bowl, whisk together flour, baking powder, baking soda, and salt. In another large bowl, cream together softened butter and granulated sugar until light and fluffy. Add eggs one at a time, beating well after each addition. Stir in vanilla extract. Gradually add the dry ingredients to the wet ingredients, alternating with sour cream and milk. Mix until just combined, then fold in the mini chocolate chips.

Fill Cupcake Liners:
- Divide the batter evenly among the cupcake liners, filling each about two-thirds full.

Bake Cupcakes:
- Bake in the preheated oven for 18-20 minutes or until a toothpick inserted into the center comes out clean. Allow cupcakes to cool completely.

Make Cookie Dough Filling:
- In a bowl, beat together softened butter and brown sugar until creamy. Add flour and salt, mixing until well combined. Fold in mini chocolate chips.

Create Well in Cupcakes:
- Use a cupcake corer or a knife to create a well in the center of each cupcake.

Fill with Cookie Dough Filling:
- Spoon or pipe the cookie dough filling into the well of each cupcake.

Make Cookie Dough Frosting:
- In a large bowl, beat together softened butter and brown sugar until creamy. Add powdered sugar, flour, salt, milk, and vanilla extract. Mix until smooth and fluffy. Fold in mini chocolate chips.

Frost Cupcakes:
- Once the cupcakes are filled, pipe or spread the cookie dough frosting on top.

Serve and Enjoy:
- Once frosted, serve and indulge in these decadent chocolate chip cookie dough cupcakes!

Tips:

- Ensure the cookie dough filling is soft enough to be easily piped or spooned into the cupcakes.
- Adjust the amount of chocolate chips in the cupcake batter, cookie dough filling, and frosting according to your preference.
- For an extra touch, drizzle with melted chocolate or sprinkle extra mini chocolate chips on top.

These chocolate chip cookie dough cupcakes offer the classic combination of a chocolate chip cupcake with a delightful cookie dough filling and frosting. Enjoy the flavors of chocolate and cookie dough in every bite, creating a delicious treat that's sure to satisfy your sweet tooth!

Lemon Blueberry Swirl Cupcakes

Ingredients:

Lemon Cupcake Batter:

- 1 1/2 cups all-purpose flour
- 1 1/2 teaspoons baking powder
- 1/4 teaspoon baking soda
- 1/4 teaspoon salt
- 1/2 cup unsalted butter, softened
- 1 cup granulated sugar
- 2 large eggs
- 1 teaspoon vanilla extract
- Zest of 1 lemon
- 1/4 cup fresh lemon juice
- 1/2 cup buttermilk

Blueberry Swirl Filling:

- 1 cup fresh or frozen blueberries
- 2 tablespoons granulated sugar
- 1 tablespoon lemon juice

Lemon Cream Cheese Frosting:

- 8 oz cream cheese, softened
- 1/2 cup unsalted butter, softened
- 4 cups powdered sugar
- Zest of 1 lemon
- 2 tablespoons fresh lemon juice
- Fresh blueberries for garnish (optional)

Instructions:

Preheat Oven and Prepare Cupcake Liners:
- Preheat your oven to 350°F (175°C). Line a muffin tin with cupcake liners.

Make Lemon Cupcake Batter:
- In a bowl, whisk together flour, baking powder, baking soda, and salt. In another large bowl, cream together softened butter and granulated sugar

until light and fluffy. Add eggs one at a time, beating well after each addition. Stir in vanilla extract, lemon zest, and lemon juice. Gradually add the dry ingredients to the wet ingredients, alternating with buttermilk. Mix until just combined.

Prepare Blueberry Swirl Filling:
- In a small saucepan, combine blueberries, sugar, and lemon juice. Cook over medium heat, stirring occasionally, until the blueberries burst and the mixture thickens. Remove from heat and let it cool.

Fill Cupcake Liners:
- Spoon the lemon cupcake batter into each cupcake liner, filling each about halfway.

Add Blueberry Swirl:
- Add a small spoonful of the blueberry swirl filling on top of the lemon batter in each cupcake liner.

Swirl with Toothpick:
- Use a toothpick or skewer to swirl the blueberry filling into the lemon batter, creating a marbled effect.

Bake Cupcakes:
- Bake in the preheated oven for 18-20 minutes or until a toothpick inserted into the center comes out clean. Allow cupcakes to cool completely.

Make Lemon Cream Cheese Frosting:
- In a large bowl, beat together softened cream cheese, softened butter, powdered sugar, lemon zest, and lemon juice until smooth and creamy.

Frost Cupcakes:
- Once the cupcakes are completely cooled, pipe or spread the lemon cream cheese frosting on top.

Garnish with Fresh Blueberries (Optional):
- Optionally, garnish each cupcake with a few fresh blueberries on top.

Serve and Enjoy:
- Once frosted and garnished, serve and enjoy these delightful lemon blueberry swirl cupcakes!

Tips:

- If using frozen blueberries for the swirl, thaw and drain any excess liquid before cooking.
- Adjust the amount of lemon zest and juice in the frosting to suit your preference for a more or less tangy flavor.

- For a burst of freshness, fold additional fresh blueberries into the cupcake batter before baking.

These lemon blueberry swirl cupcakes bring together the bright citrus flavor of lemon with the sweetness of blueberries, creating a visually stunning and delicious treat. Enjoy the harmonious combination of flavors in every bite!

Raspberry Almond Muffins

Ingredients:

Muffin Batter:

- 1 1/2 cups all-purpose flour
- 1/2 cup almond flour
- 2 teaspoons baking powder
- 1/4 teaspoon baking soda
- 1/4 teaspoon salt
- 1/2 cup unsalted butter, softened
- 1 cup granulated sugar
- 2 large eggs
- 1 teaspoon almond extract
- 1/2 teaspoon vanilla extract
- 1/2 cup sour cream
- 1/2 cup milk
- 1 1/2 cups fresh raspberries

Almond Streusel Topping:

- 1/2 cup almond flour
- 1/4 cup granulated sugar
- 2 tablespoons unsalted butter, cold and cubed
- 1/4 cup sliced almonds

Instructions:

Preheat Oven and Prepare Muffin Tin:
- Preheat your oven to 375°F (190°C). Line a muffin tin with paper liners.

Make Almond Streusel Topping:
- In a bowl, combine almond flour, sugar, and cold cubed butter. Use your fingers to mix until crumbly. Stir in sliced almonds. Set aside.

Make Muffin Batter:
- In a bowl, whisk together all-purpose flour, almond flour, baking powder, baking soda, and salt. In another large bowl, cream together softened

butter and granulated sugar until light and fluffy. Add eggs one at a time, beating well after each addition. Stir in almond extract and vanilla extract. Mix in sour cream and milk. Gradually add the dry ingredients to the wet ingredients, mixing until just combined. Gently fold in fresh raspberries.

Fill Muffin Cups:
- Divide the batter evenly among the muffin cups, filling each about two-thirds full.

Sprinkle Streusel Topping:
- Sprinkle the almond streusel topping over the muffin batter in each cup.

Bake Muffins:
- Bake in the preheated oven for 20-22 minutes or until a toothpick inserted into the center comes out clean. Allow muffins to cool in the tin for 5 minutes, then transfer them to a wire rack to cool completely.

Serve and Enjoy:
- Once cooled, serve and enjoy these delightful raspberry almond muffins!

Tips:

- Ensure the butter for the streusel topping is cold for a crumbly texture.
- Use fresh raspberries for the best flavor and texture, but if using frozen raspberries, thaw and drain them before folding into the batter.
- Adjust the amount of almond extract in the batter according to your preference for a more or less pronounced almond flavor.

These raspberry almond muffins offer a delightful combination of nutty almond flavor and the sweet-tartness of fresh raspberries. Topped with a crunchy almond streusel, they make a perfect treat for breakfast or a delightful snack. Enjoy the wonderful blend of almond and raspberry in each delicious bite!

Cinnamon Roll Cupcakes

Ingredients:

Cupcake Batter:

- 1 1/2 cups all-purpose flour
- 1 1/2 teaspoons baking powder
- 1/4 teaspoon baking soda
- 1/4 teaspoon salt
- 1/2 cup unsalted butter, softened
- 1 cup granulated sugar
- 2 large eggs
- 1 teaspoon vanilla extract
- 1/2 cup sour cream
- 1/2 cup milk

Cinnamon Filling:

- 1/4 cup unsalted butter, melted
- 1/3 cup packed brown sugar
- 1 tablespoon ground cinnamon

Cream Cheese Frosting:

- 4 oz cream cheese, softened
- 1/4 cup unsalted butter, softened
- 2 cups powdered sugar

- 1 teaspoon vanilla extract

Instructions:

Preheat Oven and Prepare Cupcake Liners:

- Preheat your oven to 350°F (175°C). Line a muffin tin with cupcake liners.

Make Cupcake Batter:

- In a bowl, whisk together flour, baking powder, baking soda, and salt. In another large bowl, cream together softened butter and granulated sugar until light and fluffy. Add eggs one at a time, beating well after each addition. Stir in vanilla extract. Mix in sour cream and milk. Gradually add the dry ingredients to the wet ingredients, mixing until just combined.

Prepare Cinnamon Filling:

- In a small bowl, combine melted butter, brown sugar, and ground cinnamon. Mix until well combined.

Fill Cupcake Liners:

- Spoon a small amount of the cupcake batter into each cupcake liner, filling each about one-third full.

Add Cinnamon Filling:

- Add a small spoonful of the cinnamon filling on top of the cupcake batter in each liner.

Top with More Batter:

- Cover the cinnamon filling with more cupcake batter, filling each cup almost to the top.

Swirl with Toothpick:

- Use a toothpick or skewer to swirl the cinnamon filling into the cupcake batter, creating a marbled effect.

Bake Cupcakes:
- Bake in the preheated oven for 18-20 minutes or until a toothpick inserted into the center comes out clean. Allow cupcakes to cool completely.

Make Cream Cheese Frosting:
- In a large bowl, beat together softened cream cheese, softened butter, powdered sugar, and vanilla extract until smooth and creamy.

Frost Cupcakes:
- Once the cupcakes are completely cooled, pipe or spread the cream cheese frosting on top.

Serve and Enjoy:
- Once frosted, serve and savor these delicious cinnamon roll cupcakes!

Tips:

- Use a toothpick or skewer to check the doneness of the cupcakes; it should come out clean when inserted into the center.
- Adjust the amount of cinnamon in the filling based on your preference for a more or less cinnamon flavor.
- For an extra touch, drizzle the cream cheese frosting with a bit of honey or maple syrup.

These cinnamon roll cupcakes capture the essence of classic cinnamon rolls in a delightful handheld treat. Enjoy the swirls of cinnamon filling and the rich cream cheese frosting for a comforting and delicious experience reminiscent of your favorite bakery cinnamon rolls!

S'mores Muffins

Ingredients:

Muffin Batter:

- 1 1/2 cups all-purpose flour
- 1/2 cup graham cracker crumbs
- 1/2 cup unsweetened cocoa powder
- 1 teaspoon baking powder
- 1/2 teaspoon baking soda
- 1/4 teaspoon salt
- 1/2 cup unsalted butter, softened
- 1 cup granulated sugar
- 2 large eggs
- 1 teaspoon vanilla extract
- 1 cup buttermilk

S'mores Filling:

- 1/2 cup chocolate chips
- 1/2 cup mini marshmallows

Graham Cracker Streusel Topping:

- 1/4 cup graham cracker crumbs
- 2 tablespoons brown sugar
- 2 tablespoons unsalted butter, melted

Additional Toppings:

- Chocolate ganache (optional)
- Mini marshmallows (for garnish)

Instructions:

Preheat Oven and Prepare Muffin Tin:
- Preheat your oven to 350°F (175°C). Line a muffin tin with paper liners.

Make Muffin Batter:

- In a bowl, whisk together flour, graham cracker crumbs, cocoa powder, baking powder, baking soda, and salt. In another large bowl, cream together softened butter and granulated sugar until light and fluffy. Add eggs one at a time, beating well after each addition. Stir in vanilla extract. Gradually add the dry ingredients to the wet ingredients, alternating with buttermilk. Mix until just combined.

Prepare Graham Cracker Streusel Topping:
- In a small bowl, combine graham cracker crumbs, brown sugar, and melted butter. Mix until well combined.

Fill Muffin Cups:
- Spoon the muffin batter into each cupcake liner, filling each about two-thirds full.

Add S'mores Filling:
- Press a few chocolate chips and mini marshmallows into the center of each muffin.

Sprinkle Streusel Topping:
- Sprinkle the graham cracker streusel topping over the muffin batter in each cup.

Bake Muffins:
- Bake in the preheated oven for 18-20 minutes or until a toothpick inserted into the center comes out clean. Allow muffins to cool in the tin for 5 minutes, then transfer them to a wire rack to cool completely.

Optional: Drizzle with Chocolate Ganache:
- If desired, drizzle cooled muffins with chocolate ganache for an extra chocolatey touch.

Garnish with Mini Marshmallows (Optional):
- Optionally, garnish each muffin with a few mini marshmallows.

Serve and Enjoy:
- Once cooled, serve and indulge in these scrumptious s'mores muffins!

Tips:

- Ensure the chocolate chips and mini marshmallows are evenly distributed in the muffin batter.
- Adjust the amount of graham cracker streusel based on your preference for a more or less crumbly topping.
- To make chocolate ganache, heat equal parts of heavy cream and chocolate until smooth and well combined.

These s'mores muffins capture the essence of the classic campfire treat with the combination of chocolate, graham cracker, and marshmallow. Enjoy the gooey marshmallow and chocolate-filled center, complemented by the graham cracker streusel topping. A delightful twist on the beloved s'mores experience!

Unique and Creative:
Margarita Cupcakes

Ingredients:

Cupcake Batter:

- 1 1/2 cups all-purpose flour
- 1 1/2 teaspoons baking powder
- 1/4 teaspoon salt
- 1/2 cup unsalted butter, softened
- 1 cup granulated sugar
- 2 large eggs
- Zest of 2 limes
- 2 tablespoons lime juice
- 1/4 cup tequila
- 1/4 cup milk

Tequila Lime Syrup:

- 1/4 cup tequila
- 1/4 cup lime juice
- 1/4 cup granulated sugar

Tequila Lime Frosting:

- 1 cup unsalted butter, softened
- 4 cups powdered sugar
- Zest of 1 lime
- 3 tablespoons lime juice
- 2 tablespoons tequila
- Lime slices for garnish (optional)

Instructions:

Preheat Oven and Prepare Cupcake Liners:
- Preheat your oven to 350°F (175°C). Line a muffin tin with cupcake liners.

Make Cupcake Batter:

- In a bowl, whisk together flour, baking powder, and salt. In another large bowl, cream together softened butter and granulated sugar until light and fluffy. Add eggs one at a time, beating well after each addition. Stir in lime zest, lime juice, tequila, and milk. Gradually add the dry ingredients to the wet ingredients, mixing until just combined.

Fill Cupcake Liners:
- Spoon the cupcake batter into each cupcake liner, filling each about two-thirds full.

Bake Cupcakes:
- Bake in the preheated oven for 18-20 minutes or until a toothpick inserted into the center comes out clean. Allow cupcakes to cool in the tin for 5 minutes, then transfer them to a wire rack to cool completely.

Make Tequila Lime Syrup:
- In a small saucepan, combine tequila, lime juice, and granulated sugar. Heat over medium heat, stirring until the sugar dissolves. Remove from heat and let it cool.

Brush Cupcakes with Syrup:
- Once the cupcakes are completely cooled, use a pastry brush to brush the tequila lime syrup over the tops of each cupcake, allowing it to soak in.

Make Tequila Lime Frosting:
- In a large bowl, beat together softened butter, powdered sugar, lime zest, lime juice, and tequila until smooth and creamy.

Frost Cupcakes:
- Pipe or spread the tequila lime frosting on top of each cupcake.

Garnish with Lime Slices (Optional):
- Optionally, garnish each cupcake with a slice of lime for decoration.

Serve and Enjoy:
- Once frosted and garnished, serve and enjoy these refreshing margarita cupcakes!

Tips:

- Adjust the amount of tequila in the syrup and frosting based on your preference for a stronger or milder tequila flavor.
- For a fun twist, rim the edges of the cupcakes with coarse salt before frosting.
- Ensure the cupcakes are completely cooled before brushing them with the tequila lime syrup to prevent sogginess.

These margarita cupcakes capture the essence of the classic cocktail with the zesty flavors of lime and a hint of tequila. Perfect for a festive occasion or a summery treat, these cupcakes offer a delightful balance of sweetness and citrusy tang. Enjoy the refreshing taste of a margarita in a cupcake form!

Caramel Macchiato Cupcakes

Ingredients:

Cupcake Batter:

- 1 1/2 cups all-purpose flour
- 1 1/2 teaspoons baking powder
- 1/4 teaspoon baking soda
- 1/4 teaspoon salt
- 1/2 cup unsalted butter, softened
- 1 cup granulated sugar
- 2 large eggs
- 1 teaspoon vanilla extract
- 1/2 cup sour cream
- 1/2 cup strong brewed coffee, cooled

Caramel Sauce:

- 1 cup granulated sugar
- 6 tablespoons unsalted butter, cut into pieces
- 1/2 cup heavy cream
- 1 teaspoon vanilla extract
- Pinch of salt

Coffee Buttercream Frosting:

- 1 cup unsalted butter, softened
- 3 cups powdered sugar
- 2 tablespoons strong brewed coffee, cooled
- 1 teaspoon vanilla extract
- Caramel sauce (for drizzling)
- Coffee beans for garnish (optional)

Instructions:

Preheat Oven and Prepare Cupcake Liners:

- Preheat your oven to 350°F (175°C). Line a muffin tin with cupcake liners.

Make Cupcake Batter:
- In a bowl, whisk together flour, baking powder, baking soda, and salt. In another large bowl, cream together softened butter and granulated sugar until light and fluffy. Add eggs one at a time, beating well after each addition. Stir in vanilla extract. Mix in sour cream and brewed coffee. Gradually add the dry ingredients to the wet ingredients, mixing until just combined.

Fill Cupcake Liners:
- Spoon the cupcake batter into each cupcake liner, filling each about two-thirds full.

Bake Cupcakes:
- Bake in the preheated oven for 18-20 minutes or until a toothpick inserted into the center comes out clean. Allow cupcakes to cool in the tin for 5 minutes, then transfer them to a wire rack to cool completely.

Make Caramel Sauce:
- In a saucepan over medium heat, melt granulated sugar, stirring constantly until it becomes a deep amber color. Add butter and stir until melted. Slowly pour in the heavy cream while stirring constantly. Remove from heat and stir in vanilla extract and a pinch of salt. Let the caramel sauce cool.

Core Cupcakes and Fill with Caramel:
- Use a cupcake corer or a knife to create a well in the center of each cupcake. Fill each well with a spoonful of cooled caramel sauce.

Make Coffee Buttercream Frosting:
- In a large bowl, beat together softened butter, powdered sugar, brewed coffee, and vanilla extract until smooth and fluffy.

Frost Cupcakes:
- Pipe or spread the coffee buttercream frosting on top of each cupcake.

Drizzle with Caramel and Garnish:
- Drizzle additional caramel sauce over the frosting and garnish with coffee beans if desired.

Serve and Enjoy:
- Once frosted, serve and savor these delicious caramel macchiato cupcakes!

Tips:

- Ensure the brewed coffee for the cupcakes and frosting is completely cooled to room temperature.
- Adjust the sweetness of the frosting by adding more or less powdered sugar according to your preference.
- For an extra touch, sprinkle a pinch of sea salt over the caramel drizzle on top.

These caramel macchiato cupcakes bring the rich flavors of coffee and caramel together in a delightful treat. With a coffee-infused cupcake, a gooey caramel center, and a coffee buttercream frosting, they offer a decadent experience reminiscent of your favorite coffeehouse drink. Enjoy the indulgent combination of sweet and coffee goodness!

Chai Spiced Muffins

Ingredients:

Chai Spice Blend:

- 2 teaspoons ground cinnamon
- 1 teaspoon ground ginger
- 1/2 teaspoon ground cardamom
- 1/4 teaspoon ground cloves
- 1/4 teaspoon ground nutmeg
- 1/4 teaspoon ground black pepper

Muffin Batter:

- 2 cups all-purpose flour
- 1 cup granulated sugar
- 1 tablespoon baking powder
- 1/2 teaspoon baking soda
- 1/2 teaspoon salt
- 1/2 cup unsalted butter, melted and cooled
- 2 large eggs
- 1 cup buttermilk
- 1 teaspoon vanilla extract
- 2 tablespoons chai spice blend (from above)

Chai Glaze:

- 1 cup powdered sugar
- 2 tablespoons brewed chai tea, cooled
- 1/2 teaspoon vanilla extract

Instructions:

Preheat Oven and Prepare Muffin Tin:
- Preheat your oven to 375°F (190°C). Line a muffin tin with paper liners.

Make Chai Spice Blend:
- In a small bowl, mix together ground cinnamon, ground ginger, ground cardamom, ground cloves, ground nutmeg, and ground black pepper. Set aside.

Make Muffin Batter:
- In a large bowl, whisk together flour, granulated sugar, baking powder, baking soda, and salt. In another bowl, whisk together melted butter, eggs, buttermilk, vanilla extract, and 2 tablespoons of the chai spice blend. Add the wet ingredients to the dry ingredients and stir until just combined.

Fill Muffin Cups:
- Spoon the muffin batter into each cupcake liner, filling each about two-thirds full.

Bake Muffins:
- Bake in the preheated oven for 18-20 minutes or until a toothpick inserted into the center comes out clean. Allow muffins to cool in the tin for 5 minutes, then transfer them to a wire rack to cool completely.

Make Chai Glaze:
- In a bowl, whisk together powdered sugar, brewed chai tea, and vanilla extract until smooth.

Drizzle with Chai Glaze:
- Once the muffins are completely cooled, drizzle the chai glaze over the top of each muffin.

Serve and Enjoy:
- Once glazed, serve and enjoy these delightful chai spiced muffins!

Tips:

- Adjust the amount of chai spice in the glaze to suit your preference for a more or less intense chai flavor.
- If you don't have buttermilk, you can make a substitute by adding 1 tablespoon of white vinegar or lemon juice to a cup of milk and letting it sit for 5 minutes before using.
- Sprinkle a little extra chai spice on top of the glaze for added visual appeal.

These chai spiced muffins offer a warm and aromatic blend of chai spices, creating a comforting and flavorful treat. With the addition of a chai glaze, these muffins are sure to please anyone who enjoys the rich and aromatic flavors of chai tea. Enjoy the cozy goodness of chai in muffin form!

Bacon Maple Pancake Cupcakes

Ingredients:

Pancake Batter:

- 1 cup all-purpose flour
- 1 tablespoon granulated sugar
- 1 teaspoon baking powder
- 1/2 teaspoon baking soda
- 1/4 teaspoon salt
- 3/4 cup buttermilk
- 1 large egg
- 2 tablespoons unsalted butter, melted
- 1 teaspoon vanilla extract

Maple Buttercream Frosting:

- 1 cup unsalted butter, softened
- 2 cups powdered sugar
- 1/4 cup pure maple syrup
- 1 teaspoon vanilla extract

Toppings:

- Cooked and crumbled bacon
- Maple syrup for drizzling

Instructions:

Preheat Oven and Prepare Cupcake Liners:
- Preheat your oven to 350°F (175°C). Line a muffin tin with cupcake liners.

Make Pancake Batter:
- In a bowl, whisk together flour, sugar, baking powder, baking soda, and salt. In another bowl, whisk together buttermilk, egg, melted butter, and vanilla extract. Add the wet ingredients to the dry ingredients and stir until just combined.

Fill Cupcake Liners:
- Spoon the pancake batter into each cupcake liner, filling each about two-thirds full.

Bake Cupcakes:
- Bake in the preheated oven for 12-15 minutes or until a toothpick inserted into the center comes out clean. Allow cupcakes to cool in the tin for 5 minutes, then transfer them to a wire rack to cool completely.

Make Maple Buttercream Frosting:
- In a large bowl, beat together softened butter, powdered sugar, maple syrup, and vanilla extract until smooth and fluffy.

Frost Cupcakes:
- Pipe or spread the maple buttercream frosting on top of each cupcake.

Top with Bacon and Drizzle with Maple Syrup:
- Sprinkle each cupcake with cooked and crumbled bacon. Drizzle with maple syrup for added flavor.

Serve and Enjoy:
- Once topped, serve and enjoy these indulgent bacon maple pancake cupcakes!

Tips:

- Ensure the bacon is cooked until crispy before crumbling it for the topping.
- Adjust the sweetness of the frosting by adding more or less powdered sugar according to your preference.
- For an extra touch, place a small pancake or a piece of bacon on top of each cupcake as a garnish.

These bacon maple pancake cupcakes combine the best of breakfast and dessert. With a pancake base, maple buttercream frosting, and crispy bacon on top, they offer a delightful and indulgent treat reminiscent of a classic breakfast. Enjoy the sweet and savory goodness of bacon and maple in cupcake form!

Sweet Potato Pecan Cupcakes

Ingredients:

Cupcake Batter:

- 1 cup all-purpose flour
- 1 teaspoon baking powder
- 1/2 teaspoon baking soda
- 1/4 teaspoon salt
- 1 teaspoon ground cinnamon
- 1/2 teaspoon ground nutmeg
- 1/4 teaspoon ground ginger
- 1/2 cup unsalted butter, softened
- 1/2 cup granulated sugar
- 1/2 cup packed light brown sugar
- 2 large eggs
- 1 cup mashed sweet potatoes (cooked and cooled)
- 1 teaspoon vanilla extract

Pecan Streusel Topping:

- 1/2 cup chopped pecans
- 1/4 cup packed light brown sugar
- 1 tablespoon all-purpose flour
- 1 tablespoon unsalted butter, melted

Cream Cheese Frosting:

- 8 oz cream cheese, softened
- 1/2 cup unsalted butter, softened
- 3 cups powdered sugar
- 1 teaspoon vanilla extract

Additional Pecans for Garnish (optional)

Instructions:

Preheat Oven and Prepare Cupcake Liners:
- Preheat your oven to 350°F (175°C). Line a muffin tin with cupcake liners.

Make Cupcake Batter:
- In a bowl, whisk together flour, baking powder, baking soda, salt, cinnamon, nutmeg, and ginger. In another large bowl, cream together softened butter, granulated sugar, and brown sugar until light and fluffy. Add eggs one at a time, beating well after each addition. Stir in mashed sweet potatoes and vanilla extract. Gradually add the dry ingredients to the wet ingredients, mixing until just combined.

Fill Cupcake Liners:
- Spoon the cupcake batter into each cupcake liner, filling each about two-thirds full.

Make Pecan Streusel Topping:
- In a small bowl, combine chopped pecans, brown sugar, flour, and melted butter. Mix until well combined.

Top with Pecan Streusel:
- Sprinkle the pecan streusel topping over the cupcake batter in each cup.

Bake Cupcakes:
- Bake in the preheated oven for 18-20 minutes or until a toothpick inserted into the center comes out clean. Allow cupcakes to cool in the tin for 5 minutes, then transfer them to a wire rack to cool completely.

Make Cream Cheese Frosting:
- In a large bowl, beat together softened cream cheese, softened butter, powdered sugar, and vanilla extract until smooth and creamy.

Frost Cupcakes:
- Pipe or spread the cream cheese frosting on top of each cupcake.

Garnish with Pecans (Optional):
- Optionally, garnish each cupcake with a pecan half for decoration.

Serve and Enjoy:
- Once frosted and garnished, serve and enjoy these delectable sweet potato pecan cupcakes!

Tips:

- Ensure the sweet potatoes are cooked and cooled before mashing them for the cupcake batter.
- Adjust the sweetness of the frosting by adding more or less powdered sugar according to your preference.

- For added flavor, consider adding a pinch of cinnamon or nutmeg to the cream cheese frosting.

These sweet potato pecan cupcakes offer a delightful blend of warm spices, sweet potatoes, and crunchy pecans. Topped with a creamy cream cheese frosting, they make for a perfect autumn treat or a festive dessert. Enjoy the rich and comforting flavors of sweet potato and pecan in each bite!

Cucumber Mint Cupcakes with Gin Frosting

Ingredients:

Cupcake Batter:

- 1 1/2 cups all-purpose flour
- 1 1/2 teaspoons baking powder
- 1/4 teaspoon salt
- 1/2 cup unsalted butter, softened
- 1 cup granulated sugar
- 2 large eggs
- 1 teaspoon vanilla extract
- 1/2 cup finely chopped cucumber (peeled and seeds removed)
- 1/4 cup finely chopped fresh mint
- 1/2 cup milk

Gin Frosting:

- 1 cup unsalted butter, softened
- 3 cups powdered sugar
- 2 tablespoons gin
- 1 teaspoon lime zest
- Fresh mint leaves and cucumber slices for garnish

Instructions:

Preheat Oven and Prepare Cupcake Liners:
- Preheat your oven to 350°F (175°C). Line a muffin tin with cupcake liners.

Make Cupcake Batter:
- In a bowl, whisk together flour, baking powder, and salt. In another large bowl, cream together softened butter and granulated sugar until light and fluffy. Add eggs one at a time, beating well after each addition. Stir in vanilla extract. Add finely chopped cucumber and fresh mint to the wet ingredients. Gradually add the dry ingredients to the wet ingredients, alternating with milk. Mix until just combined.

Fill Cupcake Liners:
- Spoon the cupcake batter into each cupcake liner, filling each about two-thirds full.

Bake Cupcakes:
- Bake in the preheated oven for 18-20 minutes or until a toothpick inserted into the center comes out clean. Allow cupcakes to cool in the tin for 5 minutes, then transfer them to a wire rack to cool completely.

Make Gin Frosting:
- In a large bowl, beat together softened butter, powdered sugar, gin, and lime zest until smooth and creamy.

Frost Cupcakes:
- Pipe or spread the gin frosting on top of each cupcake.

Garnish with Mint and Cucumber:
- Garnish each cupcake with a fresh mint leaf and a slice of cucumber for a decorative touch.

Serve and Enjoy:
- Once frosted and garnished, serve and enjoy these refreshing cucumber mint cupcakes with a hint of gin!

Tips:

- Ensure the cucumber is finely chopped to avoid large chunks in the cupcake batter.
- Adjust the amount of gin in the frosting based on your preference for a more or less pronounced gin flavor.
- For an extra burst of flavor, you can brush the cooled cupcakes with a light layer of additional gin before frosting.

These cucumber mint cupcakes with gin frosting offer a unique and refreshing flavor combination. The subtle cucumber and mint in the cupcake, paired with the aromatic gin frosting, create a delightful treat with a touch of sophistication. Enjoy these cupcakes for a light and refreshing dessert or a special occasion!

Gluten-Free and Vegan Options:

Gluten-Free Blueberry Almond Muffins

Ingredients:

- 1 1/2 cups gluten-free all-purpose flour
- 1/2 cup almond flour
- 2 teaspoons baking powder
- 1/2 teaspoon baking soda
- 1/4 teaspoon salt
- 1/2 cup unsalted butter, melted and cooled
- 1/2 cup granulated sugar
- 2 large eggs
- 1 teaspoon vanilla extract
- 1 cup plain yogurt (or Greek yogurt)
- 1 1/2 cups fresh blueberries

Almond Streusel Topping:

- 1/4 cup almond flour
- 2 tablespoons brown sugar
- 2 tablespoons sliced almonds
- 2 tablespoons unsalted butter, melted

Instructions:

Preheat Oven and Prepare Muffin Liners:
- Preheat your oven to 350°F (175°C). Line a muffin tin with paper liners.

Make Almond Streusel Topping:
- In a small bowl, combine almond flour, brown sugar, sliced almonds, and melted butter. Mix until the ingredients form a crumbly streusel topping. Set aside.

Make Muffin Batter:
- In a medium bowl, whisk together gluten-free all-purpose flour, almond flour, baking powder, baking soda, and salt. In another large bowl, whisk together melted butter and granulated sugar until well combined. Add eggs one at a time, beating well after each addition. Stir in vanilla extract. Gradually add the dry ingredients to the wet ingredients, alternating with the yogurt. Mix until just combined. Gently fold in fresh blueberries.

Fill Muffin Liners:
- Spoon the muffin batter into each cupcake liner, filling each about two-thirds full.

Sprinkle Streusel Topping:
- Sprinkle the almond streusel topping over the muffin batter in each cup.

Bake Muffins:
- Bake in the preheated oven for 18-20 minutes or until a toothpick inserted into the center comes out clean. Allow muffins to cool in the tin for 5 minutes, then transfer them to a wire rack to cool completely.

Serve and Enjoy:
- Once cooled, serve and enjoy these gluten-free blueberry almond muffins with a delightful almond streusel topping!

Tips:

- Ensure all your ingredients are labeled gluten-free to maintain a gluten-free recipe.
- If using frozen blueberries, toss them in a little bit of gluten-free flour before folding them into the batter to prevent them from sinking to the bottom of the muffins.
- Adjust the sweetness by adding more or less sugar to the batter according to your preference.

These gluten-free blueberry almond muffins offer a tender crumb, bursting with juicy blueberries and topped with a nutty almond streusel. Perfect for those who follow a gluten-free diet or anyone looking for a delicious and wholesome muffin option. Enjoy the delightful combination of blueberries and almonds in each bite!

Vegan Chocolate Chip Banana Muffins

Ingredients:

- 2 ripe bananas, mashed
- 1/2 cup unsweetened applesauce
- 1/4 cup melted coconut oil or vegetable oil
- 1/2 cup granulated sugar
- 1 teaspoon vanilla extract
- 1 1/2 cups all-purpose flour
- 1 teaspoon baking soda
- 1/2 teaspoon baking powder
- 1/4 teaspoon salt
- 1/2 cup vegan chocolate chips (plus extra for topping)

Instructions:

Preheat Oven and Prepare Muffin Liners:
- Preheat your oven to 350°F (175°C). Line a muffin tin with paper liners.

Make Banana Muffin Batter:
- In a large mixing bowl, combine mashed bananas, applesauce, melted coconut oil, granulated sugar, and vanilla extract. Mix until well combined.

Add Dry Ingredients:
- In a separate bowl, whisk together flour, baking soda, baking powder, and salt. Gradually add the dry ingredients to the wet ingredients, mixing until just combined. Be careful not to overmix.

Fold in Chocolate Chips:
- Gently fold in the vegan chocolate chips until evenly distributed throughout the batter.

Fill Muffin Liners:
- Spoon the muffin batter into each cupcake liner, filling each about two-thirds full.

Top with Chocolate Chips:
- Sprinkle a few extra chocolate chips on top of each muffin for a decorative touch.

Bake Muffins:

- Bake in the preheated oven for 18-20 minutes or until a toothpick inserted into the center comes out clean. Allow muffins to cool in the tin for 5 minutes, then transfer them to a wire rack to cool completely.

Serve and Enjoy:
- Once cooled, serve and enjoy these delicious vegan chocolate chip banana muffins!

Tips:

- Make sure to use ripe bananas for enhanced sweetness and flavor.
- You can substitute other plant-based oils such as olive oil or canola oil for the coconut oil.
- If you prefer, you can add chopped nuts, such as walnuts or pecans, to the batter for extra texture.

These vegan chocolate chip banana muffins are a delightful and plant-based twist on a classic favorite. The combination of ripe bananas and chocolate chips creates a moist and flavorful muffin that is perfect for breakfast, a snack, or a sweet treat any time of the day. Enjoy the goodness of vegan baking with these delicious muffins!

Gluten-Free Lemon Coconut Cupcakes

Ingredients:

Cupcake Batter:

- 1 1/2 cups gluten-free all-purpose flour
- 1/2 cup desiccated coconut
- 1 1/2 teaspoons baking powder
- 1/2 teaspoon baking soda
- 1/4 teaspoon salt
- 1/2 cup unsalted butter, softened
- 1 cup granulated sugar
- 2 large eggs
- 1 teaspoon vanilla extract
- 1 tablespoon lemon zest
- 1/4 cup fresh lemon juice
- 1/2 cup coconut milk (full-fat)

Coconut Lemon Glaze:

- 1 cup powdered sugar
- 2 tablespoons coconut milk
- 2 tablespoons fresh lemon juice
- Shredded coconut for topping

Instructions:

Preheat Oven and Prepare Muffin Liners:
- Preheat your oven to 350°F (175°C). Line a muffin tin with paper liners.

Make Cupcake Batter:
- In a medium bowl, whisk together gluten-free all-purpose flour, desiccated coconut, baking powder, baking soda, and salt. In another large bowl, cream together softened butter and granulated sugar until light and fluffy. Add eggs one at a time, beating well after each addition. Stir in vanilla extract, lemon zest, and fresh lemon juice. Gradually add the dry ingredients to the wet ingredients, alternating with coconut milk. Mix until just combined.

Fill Muffin Liners:

- Spoon the cupcake batter into each cupcake liner, filling each about two-thirds full.

Bake Cupcakes:
- Bake in the preheated oven for 18-20 minutes or until a toothpick inserted into the center comes out clean. Allow cupcakes to cool in the tin for 5 minutes, then transfer them to a wire rack to cool completely.

Make Coconut Lemon Glaze:
- In a bowl, whisk together powdered sugar, coconut milk, and fresh lemon juice until smooth.

Glaze Cupcakes:
- Once the cupcakes are completely cooled, drizzle the coconut lemon glaze over the top of each cupcake.

Top with Shredded Coconut:
- Sprinkle shredded coconut on top of the glaze for added texture and flavor.

Serve and Enjoy:
- Once glazed and topped, serve and enjoy these gluten-free lemon coconut cupcakes!

Tips:

- Ensure all your ingredients are labeled gluten-free to maintain a gluten-free recipe.
- Adjust the thickness of the glaze by adding more or less powdered sugar to achieve your desired consistency.
- Toast the shredded coconut for a few minutes in a dry pan for a nuttier flavor before topping the cupcakes.

These gluten-free lemon coconut cupcakes offer a bright and tropical twist to a classic treat. The combination of zesty lemon and sweet coconut creates a delightful cupcake that is perfect for any occasion. Enjoy the refreshing flavors of lemon and coconut in each bite!

Vegan Pumpkin Spice Cupcakes

Ingredients:

Cupcake Batter:

- 1 1/2 cups all-purpose flour
- 1 teaspoon baking powder
- 1/2 teaspoon baking soda
- 1/4 teaspoon salt
- 1 teaspoon ground cinnamon
- 1/2 teaspoon ground ginger
- 1/4 teaspoon ground nutmeg
- 1/4 teaspoon ground cloves
- 1 cup canned pumpkin puree
- 1/2 cup maple syrup
- 1/3 cup vegetable oil
- 1/2 cup unsweetened almond milk (or any plant-based milk)
- 1 teaspoon vanilla extract

Vegan Cream Cheese Frosting:

- 8 oz vegan cream cheese, softened
- 1/4 cup vegan butter, softened
- 3 cups powdered sugar
- 1 teaspoon vanilla extract

Optional Garnish:

- Ground cinnamon for dusting
- Pumpkin seeds for topping

Instructions:

Preheat Oven and Prepare Muffin Liners:
- Preheat your oven to 350°F (175°C). Line a muffin tin with paper liners.

Make Cupcake Batter:
- In a medium bowl, whisk together flour, baking powder, baking soda, salt, cinnamon, ginger, nutmeg, and cloves. In another large bowl, whisk together pumpkin puree, maple syrup, vegetable oil, almond milk, and

vanilla extract. Gradually add the dry ingredients to the wet ingredients, mixing until just combined.

Fill Muffin Liners:
- Spoon the cupcake batter into each cupcake liner, filling each about two-thirds full.

Bake Cupcakes:
- Bake in the preheated oven for 18-20 minutes or until a toothpick inserted into the center comes out clean. Allow cupcakes to cool in the tin for 5 minutes, then transfer them to a wire rack to cool completely.

Make Vegan Cream Cheese Frosting:
- In a large bowl, beat together softened vegan cream cheese, softened vegan butter, powdered sugar, and vanilla extract until smooth and creamy.

Frost Cupcakes:
- Pipe or spread the vegan cream cheese frosting on top of each cupcake.

Garnish (Optional):
- Dust the frosted cupcakes with ground cinnamon and top each with a few pumpkin seeds for a decorative touch.

Serve and Enjoy:
- Once frosted and garnished, serve and enjoy these delicious vegan pumpkin spice cupcakes!

Tips:

- Adjust the sweetness of the frosting by adding more or less powdered sugar according to your preference.
- For a nutty flavor, consider adding chopped pecans or walnuts to the batter or sprinkling them on top as a garnish.
- Ensure the pumpkin puree is well-mixed into the batter for an even distribution of flavor.

These vegan pumpkin spice cupcakes capture the essence of fall with warm spices and the rich taste of pumpkin. Topped with vegan cream cheese frosting, they make for a delightful treat that is perfect for autumn gatherings or any time you crave a taste of the season. Enjoy the comforting flavors of pumpkin spice in a delicious and vegan-friendly cupcake!

Gluten-Free Zucchini Chocolate Muffins

Ingredients:

- 1 1/2 cups gluten-free all-purpose flour
- 1/2 cup cocoa powder
- 1 teaspoon baking powder
- 1/2 teaspoon baking soda
- 1/4 teaspoon salt
- 1/2 cup coconut oil, melted
- 1/2 cup maple syrup or honey
- 2 large eggs
- 1 teaspoon vanilla extract
- 1 1/2 cups grated zucchini (excess moisture squeezed out)
- 1/2 cup dairy-free chocolate chips

Instructions:

Preheat Oven and Prepare Muffin Liners:
- Preheat your oven to 350°F (175°C). Line a muffin tin with paper liners.

Make Muffin Batter:
- In a medium bowl, whisk together gluten-free all-purpose flour, cocoa powder, baking powder, baking soda, and salt. In another large bowl, whisk together melted coconut oil, maple syrup (or honey), eggs, and vanilla extract. Gradually add the dry ingredients to the wet ingredients, mixing until just combined. Fold in grated zucchini and chocolate chips.

Fill Muffin Liners:
- Spoon the muffin batter into each cupcake liner, filling each about two-thirds full.

Bake Muffins:
- Bake in the preheated oven for 18-20 minutes or until a toothpick inserted into the center comes out clean. Allow muffins to cool in the tin for 5 minutes, then transfer them to a wire rack to cool completely.

Serve and Enjoy:
- Once cooled, serve and enjoy these gluten-free zucchini chocolate muffins!

Tips:

- Ensure all your ingredients are labeled gluten-free to maintain a gluten-free recipe.
- Squeeze out excess moisture from the grated zucchini using a clean kitchen towel before folding it into the batter.
- Feel free to add chopped nuts, such as walnuts or pecans, for extra texture and flavor.

These gluten-free zucchini chocolate muffins are a delicious and wholesome way to enjoy chocolatey goodness while incorporating the goodness of zucchini. The moist texture of the zucchini complements the rich chocolate flavor, making these muffins a delightful gluten-free treat. Enjoy them as a snack or a guilt-free dessert!

Vegan Vanilla Raspberry Cupcakes

Ingredients:

Cupcake Batter:

- 1 1/2 cups all-purpose flour
- 1 teaspoon baking powder
- 1/2 teaspoon baking soda
- 1/4 teaspoon salt
- 1 cup almond milk (or any plant-based milk)
- 1 teaspoon apple cider vinegar
- 1/2 cup coconut oil, melted
- 3/4 cup granulated sugar
- 2 teaspoons vanilla extract
- 1 cup fresh raspberries (or frozen, thawed)

Vegan Vanilla Frosting:

- 1/2 cup vegan butter, softened
- 2 cups powdered sugar
- 1 teaspoon vanilla extract
- 2-3 tablespoons almond milk (or any plant-based milk)

Additional Raspberries for Garnish (Optional)

Instructions:

Preheat Oven and Prepare Muffin Liners:
- Preheat your oven to 350°F (175°C). Line a muffin tin with paper liners.

Make Cupcake Batter:
- In a small bowl, combine almond milk and apple cider vinegar. Let it sit for a few minutes to create a vegan "buttermilk." In a medium bowl, whisk together all-purpose flour, baking powder, baking soda, and salt. In another large bowl, whisk together melted coconut oil, granulated sugar, vanilla extract, and the almond milk mixture. Gradually add the dry ingredients to the wet ingredients, mixing until just combined. Gently fold in fresh raspberries.

Fill Muffin Liners:

- Spoon the cupcake batter into each cupcake liner, filling each about two-thirds full.

Bake Cupcakes:
- Bake in the preheated oven for 18-20 minutes or until a toothpick inserted into the center comes out clean. Allow cupcakes to cool in the tin for 5 minutes, then transfer them to a wire rack to cool completely.

Make Vegan Vanilla Frosting:
- In a large bowl, beat together softened vegan butter, powdered sugar, vanilla extract, and almond milk until smooth and creamy.

Frost Cupcakes:
- Pipe or spread the vegan vanilla frosting on top of each cupcake.

Garnish with Raspberries (Optional):
- Optionally, garnish each cupcake with a fresh raspberry for decoration.

Serve and Enjoy:
- Once frosted and garnished, serve and enjoy these delicious vegan vanilla raspberry cupcakes!

Tips:

- If using frozen raspberries, thaw them and pat them dry with a paper towel before folding them into the batter.
- Adjust the sweetness of the frosting by adding more or less powdered sugar according to your preference.
- For a burst of lemony flavor, consider adding a teaspoon of lemon zest to the cupcake batter.

These vegan vanilla raspberry cupcakes offer a delightful combination of light and fluffy vanilla cake with bursts of juicy raspberries. Topped with vegan vanilla frosting, they make for a perfect plant-based treat that's both delicious and visually appealing. Enjoy the sweet and tangy flavors in every bite!

www.ingramcontent.com/pod-product-compliance
Lightning Source LLC
LaVergne TN
LVHW061936070526
838199LV00060B/3846